I0197600

The Economic Conditions of Judaea after the Destruction of the Second Temple

BY

ADOLPH BÜCHLER, PH.D.

PRINCIPAL OF JEWS' COLLEGE

WIPF & STOCK · Eugene, Oregon

Wipf and Stock Publishers
199 W 8th Ave, Suite 3
Eugene, OR 97401

The Economic Conditions of Judaea after the
Destruction of the Second Temple
By Buchler, Adolph
ISBN 13: 978-1-60608-687-2
Publication date 5/15/2009
Previously published by Jews' College, 1912

CONTENTS

CHAPTER I. The places and the population of Judaea preserved after the year 70 (3–29). Josephus's report in his *Wars* of places in Judaea destroyed and people killed by the Romans in the years 66 to 70, places not destroyed on the road from Caesarea to Jerusalem, east of the Jordan, in the north, west and north-west of Judaea, number of people saved by surrender and desertion from Jerusalem, noble and other deserters. Talmudic references to persons saved, priests, levites, scholars, men and women, places preserved, pilgrimage to Jerusalem continued after 70, Lydda and Jamnia populated by Vespasian in 68 by Jews from other places, some of the inhabitants, synagogues, schools, trade, places around Lydda and Jamnia and in other parts of Judaea.

CHAPTER II. Economic conditions and landed property (29–55). Land retained by deserters, leased from Vespasian by others, Talmudic material on landowners, the laws concerning tithes and priestly dues observed, wealthy scholars in Judaea, money, poor men, agriculture and its results, cattle and flocks, drought, food and drink, occupations, depressed mood of Jews, women and children.

CHAPTER III. The political conditions in Judaea and the Romans (55–68). Robbers after the war in Judaea, Roman garrisons, imperial tax-collecting stores in Jamnia, Roman courts, land in Roman possession, taxes, idolatry, other non-Jews in Judaea, conclusions.

THE ECONOMIC CONDITIONS OF JUDAEA AFTER THE DESTRUCTION OF THE SECOND TEMPLE.

I. The Places and the Population of Judaea Preserved after the Year 70.

Josephus, the contemporary historian of the Jewish war of the years 66–70, devoted a work of seven books to the events of that short period, and it should not be difficult to describe the condition in which the war left Judaea. Josephus seems rather anxious to register the rapid achievements of Vespasian, Titus, and their generals and officers, the Roman victories and the slaughter of thousands of Jews; an enumeration of all the places conquered or destroyed by the Romans could then reasonably be expected. Actually, however, the information from Josephus is rather fragmentary, though he describes the downfall of Jerusalem and reports the destruction of some parts of the trans-Jordanic country to Jericho in the western district, and in Judaea of the region from Antipatris southwards to beth-Gubrin.

1. From his fullness of material in these accounts the inference seems justified that whenever in a report of a campaign no destruction is mentioned, the towns and villages were spared by the Romans, probably in consequence of the early surrender of the defending Jews. This can be tested in his account of the way in which the Romans dealt with places on the main road from Caesarea, the residence of the governor and the starting-point of all military expeditions against Judaea, to Jerusalem, the centre of the Jewish rebellion. Owing to this geographical position Antipatris, Lydda, Emmaus, and beth-Ḥoron had to

suffer the first blows of the Roman revenge, and Josephus described fully its details. At the beginning of the revolution in the autumn of the year 66, Cestius Gallus on his march from Caesarea against Jerusalem left Antipatris without inflicting any harm (*Wars*, II, 19, 1), but owing to the hostile military preparations of some Jews in a tower near Antipatris he burnt many villages. In Lydda, a Jewish town (Philo, *Legatio* 28), he found no man, for all had gone up to Jerusalem for the feast of Tabernacles, but he killed fifty persons and burnt the town. A part of his army marched against Joppé and slaughtered all its inhabitants, 8,400 men, women, and children, plundered the town and burnt it (II, 18, 10).[1] Early in the spring of the year 68 Vespasian marched from Caesarea to Antipatris, where he spent two days to settle the affairs of the town (IV, 8, 1). On the third day he marched on and destroyed by fire and arms all the places round about. Having subdued the whole district of Thamna, he marched on Lydda and Jamnia that very soon fell into his hands, and now received as inhabitants a suitable number of such Jews as had deserted from the rebels to the Romans. Thence he went to Emmaus, where he seized the defiles which led to Jerusalem; then he passed through the district of Bethleptephai, laying it and the neighbouring district waste by fire. These statements of Josephus show that Lydda and Jamnia had been in Roman possession from 66 or 67 and were populated with loyal Jews, and that Emmaus was not destroyed.

Again, Josephus reports (IV, 9, 1) that Vespasian built a fortified camp in Adida, where he placed Romans and

[1] It remained in this condition for two years, and only after the Roman conquest of Galilee some refugees began to rebuild it (III, 9, 2), but the Romans destroyed it utterly a second time (III, 9, 3). They placed there a garrison of foot and horsemen who plundered the neighbourhood of Joppé and destroyed the neighbouring villages and townlets (II, 9, 4) and turned the whole district into a real desert. Lydda must also have been rebuilt by the Jewish general appointed after Cestius's defeat by the revolutionists for Thamna including Lydda, Joppé, and Emmaus (II, 20, 4).

soldiers of his allies. He sent Lucius Annius with a squadron of horsemen and a great number of footmen against Gerasa. The town was taken at the first attack, all young men who had not escaped in time, numbering a thousand, were killed, their families were taken captive, and all property was plundered by the soldiers. After burning the town they turned against the neighbouring villages, where all fled, the weak were destroyed, and the abandoned places burnt. In this way the whole mountainous district and the whole plain were invaded by war. Gerasa cannot mean the Hellenistic city east of the Jordan, for it would not have been hostile to the Romans, but to the Jews. The term Oreiné and the immediate reference to the position of Jerusalem suggest that this Gerasa was in the mountains north or north-west of Jerusalem,[1] and we see the destruction of many places, but at the same time the escape of their inhabitants. In Sivan of the year 69 Vespasian marched from Caesarea to subdue all the districts of Judaea not yet conquered (IV, 9, 9). He went to the mountainous country, seized upon the district of Gofna and Akrabatene, then upon the smaller towns of Bethel and Ephraim, where he placed troops. Not one word suggests that these or other places in the district were destroyed, while the necessity of garrisons indicates the strategical importance of the towns, and also the presence of a Jewish population not quite to be trusted. Cerealis, the legate of the fifth legion stationed in Emmaus (IV, 8, 1), had to subdue Upper Idumaea, the southern part of Judaea. He burnt Kafethra and besieged Kafarabis, the inhabitants of which soon surrendered and were accepted (IV, 9, 9); this means the place was spared. East of the Jordan, Gadara, the important and fortified city and inhabited by many wealthy men, asked for and in time obtained a Roman garrison from Vespasian (IV, 7, 3). One of his officers,

[1] See Reland; Kohout, *Flavius Josephus*, 660, note 487, suggests Gazara, Gezer.

Placidus, continued in the spring of the year 68 the conquest of Peraia, killed thousands of Jews (IV, 7, 4), among the first, the rebels of Gadara that had fled to Bethennabris and had found there support; then other villages with their inhabitants were destroyed, Abila, Julias, and Besimoth, and all the villages down to the Dead Sea were conquered (IV, 7, 5–6) and Jewish deserters placed there. Thus the whole district from Peraia down to Machairus had either voluntarily joined the Romans or was conquered by force. During the winter of the year 68 Vespasian put garrisons in the conquered villages and townlets and made many of the destroyed places habitable (IV, 8, 1).

2. Incidentally Josephus mentioned that Vespasian and one of his generals had settled Jews who had deserted to the Romans in Jamnia and Lydda and in some places near the mouth of the Jordan, but he says nothing about the original towns and villages of those Jews. They were no Galileans; for those who had surrendered in the course of the Galilean war, as far as can be gathered from Josephus, remained in their respective places, and no transplantation is reported. After the conquest of Galilee in the year 67 only a few Galileans left their country to join the defenders of Jerusalem. Only John of Gischala and his warriors of the same town with their families left the place immediately before its fall, and made for Jerusalem (IV, 2, 4). But 6,000 of the men were overtaken by the Romans and killed (2, 5), and 3,000 women and children were forced to return. From Judaea great multitudes under their respective leaders flocked into Jerusalem (3, 3), zealots and sicarii (3, 4), but their numbers are nowhere stated. 20,000 Idumaeans came to Jerusalem (4, 2), but most of them soon left and returned home (6, 1). As the siege of the capital in the year 70 began on the day of the Passover sacrifice (V, 13, 7, VI, 9, 3), to which naturally many thousands of pilgrims had arrived from all parts of the country, the number of

the besieged was very great. Among them were many from beyond the Euphrates and other foreign lands (*Dio Cassius*, 66, 4). 1,100,000 men perished during the siege, 97,000 were taken captive (VI, 9, 3), of these only 40,000 were preserved (8, 2), all citizens of Jerusalem (8, 2), the rest were sold for slaves, some sent into the mines in Egypt (9, 2), others distributed among the provinces for the circuses.

Considering the state of Judaea, the only questions are, which section of the citizens of Jerusalem was preserved, and where did the 40,000 settle after having been allowed to go where they liked (V, 8, 2; 10, 1)? In the course of his account of the siege Josephus several times refers to individuals who deserted to the Romans from Jerusalem, and it is not evident whether they were included in the 40,000 ultimately preserved or not. He mentions one of the four sons of the high priest Matthias (V, 13, 1), the high priests Joseph and Jesus, and three sons of the high priest Ismael, four sons of a Matthias, and many other nobles who succeeded in escaping from the besieged capital to the Romans (VI, 2, 2). Many of the eminent citizens ran away to Titus (V, 13, 7) and told him the number of the poor who had died. Titus allowed these to retire to Gofna; there, he said, they should stay till his hands would be free from the war, when he would restore to them their property. Among the numerous deserters was the priest Jesus, son of Thebuthi (VI, 8, 3), who surrendered many costly vessels of the Temple, as well as the curtains and the robe of the high priest. The treasurer of the Temple also fell into the hands of the Romans and was exceptionally pardoned in exchange for valuable stuff, priestly garments, and costly spices. Already, after Cestius's defeat in the year 66, many of the nobles had left Jerusalem as if it were a sinking ship; for instance, the two brothers Costobarus and Saul, along with Philip, son of Jakimos, who had been a general of Agrippa's troops (II, 20, 1). After the entry of the Romans into Jerusalem Titus liberated all those Jews who had been thrown into prison by the zealots (VI, 9, 1); they also most probably belonged to the wealthy section of the population.[1] It may be assumed as almost certain that the members of both groups, of the priestly and of the lay nobility of Jerusalem, received at the conclusion of the war their landed property, and assisted the poor country of Judaea in recovering from its terrible downfall. Where they settled is nowhere indicated by Josephus; he lived in Rome and seemed to evince no interest in the state of his native country after the destruction. It is possible that, though owning land in Judaea, some of the nobles settled outside Judaea, as Josephus, who, in exchange for his fields near Jerusalem, received from Titus others in the plain, and was rewarded by Vespasian by additional property in Judaea (*Vita*, 76).

3. Though no historical work in the ordinary sense, the Talmudic literature in its incidental references to conditions of life and to property contains valuable information about Judaea during the sixty-five years from the destruction of the second Temple to the war of bar-Kochba. The Halakhah deals with all details of religious life that were placed before the rabbis of that period or were discussed in the schools; but here only facts and incidents reported within those discussions will be adduced. Two high priests are referred to by R. Ishmael as testifying respectively to two different ways in which they had performed the same sacrificial act on the Day of Atonement.[2] A

[1] In *Vita*, 75, Josephus reports how he, after the conquest of Jerusalem, delivered from among the captives several men, his brother and fifty friends, and from among the great mass of women and children kept as captives in the Temple about 190 whom he had recognized as belonging to his friends and companions; he freed them without ransom. In Thekoa he saw many captives crucified, among them three of his friends who at his request were taken down, but only one survived.

[2] Baraitha in *Joma*, 59 a: two high priests survived the first Temple; one said that in the service on the Day of Atonement he had sprinkled the blood of the sin-offering on the four corners of the altar while standing in the same place, the other said that he had walked around the altar for

vice high priest, or the head of all the priests on duty, סגן הכהנים, was Ḥaninah who had officiated in the Temple[1] and survived its destruction.[2] R. Ishmael, a priest (*Ḥull.*, 49a), was the son of a high priest[3] who had worn the robe and the golden plate.[4] Simeon the Chaste told R. Eliezer that he had once entered the space behind the altar with unwashed hands and feet (*Tos. Kelim*, I, 1, 6); he was a priest. R. Ṣadok, the priest (*Bekhor.*, 36 a) who had once quieted the people assembled in the Temple and excited by the murder of a priest,[5] was, with his son Eleazar, saved by R. Joḥanan b. Zakkai from among the captives (*Threni r.*, 1, 5, *Gittin*, 56 a), and both were later friends of R. Gamaliel II in Jamnia. R. Ṣadok gave, with R. Joshua, evidence about some customs in Jerusalem (*'Eduj.*, VII, 1–4), and his son reported many interesting

the purpose of sprinkling the blood, and both gave their reasons. In the *Mishnah Joma*, V, 5, R. Eliezer holds the view of the first high priest, the same in *Baraitha Joma*, 59 a, *jer.*, V, 42 d, 62. The parallel account, *jer.*, V, 42 d, 66, reads: two priests fled in the wars, one said that he had stood, the other that he had walked while atoning. This shows, what is otherwise clear, that high priests of the second Temple are meant, as Ishmael, son of Fiabi, the best known high priest in the Talmud, who survived the destruction and was later in Kyrene (*Wars*, VI, 2, 2; in *Sotah*, IX, 15: since Ishmael b. Fiabi died, the glory of the priesthood ceased); he could have given the information quoted.

[1] Jelamdenu in *RÉJ*, 1887, XIV, 93, *Joma*, 21 b, 39 a, *'Eduj.*, II, 1–3, *Pesaḥ.*, I, 6, *Shekal.*, VI, 1.

[2] *Ta'an.*, 13 a, *jer. Beṣah*, II, 61 b, 51, and parallels.

[3] *Tos. Ḥallah*, I, 10; when he was to be executed, he said to the Roman executioner: 'I am a priest, the son of a high priest,' *ARN*, XXXVIII, 57 b, the parallels make him himself a high priest. As Samuel the Young, who died before R. Gamaliel II (*Semaḥ.*, VIII), prophesied before his death the end of R. Ishmael (*Tos. Sotah*, XIII, 4, *jer.*, IX, 24 b, 38; *Synh.*, 11 a; *Semaḥ.*, VIII; Bacher, *Tannaiten*, I, 234, 3). R. Ishmael's death seems to have been brought about by the political unrest in the year 117.

[4] A Simeon b. Jehoṣadak, a priest, died in Lydda (*Semaḥ.*, IV, 11); when his brother came from Galilee to engage in his burial and defile himself, Simeon was already buried, and the rabbis—in *Conforte R. Tarfon*—would not allow him to defile himself (Brüll, *Jahrbücher*, I, 38). As R. Tarfon's name is doubtful, most scholars take Simeon b. Jehoṣadak to be identical with R. Joḥanan's teacher in the first half of the third century (Bacher, *PA*, I, 119).

[5] *Tos. Joma*, I, 12, *jer.*, II, 39 d, 15, b. 23 a.

facts and customs which he had observed there before the year 70. Another priest, Zechariah b. haKaṣṣab, reports (*Kethub.*, II, 9) how he escaped with his wife from Jerusalem when the enemy entered the town; and we are informed of the arrangements which, on account of that, he made for his wife with whom, as a priest, he could no longer live (*Kethub.*, 27 b; *Tos.*, III, 2). Later on he gave evidence with Josê the priest, a disciple of R. Joḥanan b. Zakkai, about a point of law. R. Tarfon had once as a young priest stood on the platform in the Temple, from which the priests, among whom was his uncle, blessed the people (*Kiddush.*, 71 a), and he watched the blowing of trumpets by priests on the occasion when King Agrippa read from the Torah before the people assembled on the Temple mount (*Tos. Sotah*, VII, 16; *Sifrê Num.*, 75). After the year 70 he settled in Lydda and taught there.[1] Of high officials of the Temple, none is mentioned as surviving its destruction (see below); but R. Ishmael once met one of the grandsons of the Abtinas family who had for some time prepared the incense. R. Ishmael b. Luga told R. Akiba that he had once gathered plants with one of the grandsons, and R. Joḥanan b. Nuri told R. Akiba that he once met an old man with a scroll on the preparation of spices in his hand who belonged to the family of Abtinas.[2] The age of the last mentioned man shows that he had lived for some time before the destruction of the Temple which he survived. As the Talmud refers only incidentally to individual priests, it may be confidently assumed that many more escaped from Jerusalem and other places in Judaea. The institution of R. Joḥanan b. Zakkai, that also after the destruction of the Temple priests should

[1] R. Jehudah in *Bekhor.*, 45 b, *Tos.*, V, 7, reports how R. Tarfon said to a man with twelve fingers on his hands and twelve toes on his feet and inquiring whether he was fit (to be a priest): May, like you, many be (high) priests in Israel; according to R. Josê he said to the man: Few shall be, like you, Mamzers and Nathins in Israel. This man was a priest.

[2] *Joma*, 38 a, b, *jer.*, III, 41 a, 63; *Tos.*, II, 7.

barefooted bless the people in the synagogue (*Rosh ha-Shan.*, 31b), clearly shows the presence of priests in Jamnia. This is also evident from his other decree quoted by R. Gamaliel (*'Eduj.*, VIII, 3) that no court should be constituted to deal with the question whether a certain widow may become the wife of a priest, as priests refuse to accept the permission.[1]

Of Levites little is known. R. Joshua b. Ḥananjah had belonged to the singers in the Temple and had once wanted to assist Joḥanan b. Gudgeda in closing the gates of the Temple (*'Arakh.*, 11 b). He had at the same time been a disciple of R. Joḥanan b. Zakkai whom he helped R. Eliezer to carry from the besieged capital and with whom he escaped into the Roman camp (*ARN*, IV, 12 a, 2, VI, 10 a). After the destruction of Jerusalem, he belonged for many years to the school of Jamnia, first under R. Joḥanan and later under R. Gamaliel II, and reported several interesting details of religious practice in Jerusalem. The other Levite, Joḥanan b. Gudgeda, had belonged to the gate-keepers of the Temple (*Tos. Shekal.*, II, 14; *'Arakh.*, 11 b); he had in Jerusalem deaf mute children who were entrusted with watching the levitical purification of vessels (*jer. Terum.*, I, 40 b, 24;

[1] The priests continued to guard their purity of stock against the intrusion of tainted or doubtful families. R. Joḥanan's decree could have been issued before the year 70; but nothing is otherwise known of similar decrees of his at that time, and, from the subject-matter, it is almost certain that the ruling mentioned belongs to the period of his activity in Jamnia. And there is evidence for the same attitude of the priests even later. Rabba b. bar-Ḥanna (*Kiddush.*, 78 b) and R. Assi in R. Joḥanan's name (*jer. Bikk.*, I, 64 a, 27) remark that since the destruction of the Temple the priests have guarded their dignity by not marrying a woman both whose parents were proselytes. Other peculiarities of priests proving their number in *Baraitha Bekhor.*, 30 b, reported by R. Josê b. Ḥalaftha: since the destruction of the Temple priests have guarded their dignity by not entrusting their levitically pure food to a non-priest. In *Tos. 'Eduj.*, I, 9, it is stated that priests followed R. Ishmael's view on a point of law discussed in *'Eduj.*, II, 6. In *Tos. Ahil.*, XVI, 13, *Mikw.*, VI, 2, *Pesaḥ.*, 9 a, *jer.* i, 27 c, 39, R. Jehudah and R. Simeon b. Gamaliel report incidents in Rimmon with several priests.

Tos., I, 1). He survived the destruction of Jerusalem and gave evidence before the authorities in Jamnia about a point of law.[1]

4. Of the scholars who survived the destruction of Jerusalem R. Joḥanan b. Zakkai is to be mentioned first. He was probably a priest,[2] and had not only been the vice-president of the Synedrion beside Simeon b. Gamaliel as president, but had also fought the Sadducees in both their teachings and their practices (*Jadaj.*, IV, 6, *Tos. Parah*, III, 8). After the destruction of Jerusalem he opened a school and constituted a beth-din in Jamnia by which he created the means for the continuity and the preservation without the Temple of Judaism. As important members of this beth-din the sons of Bethera are mentioned in *Rosh haShan.*, 29 b. Though they seem to represent a whole party in the opposition, their name shows the stock to have consisted of a family that had survived the Temple, as a Joshua

[1] *Gittin*, V, 2; *'Eduj.*, VII, 9; *Jebam.*, XIV, 2, *Ḥull.*, 55 b. In *Tos. 'Arakh.*, I, 15, R. Ḥaninah b. Antigonos says that he knew certain men who had blown the flute in front of the altar in Jerusalem, and that they were Levites. Either he lived before the destruction of the Temple and survived it, or those Levites lived long after the year 70 and R. Ḥaninah met them when they were old. Now he quotes a statement of R. Eleazar Ḥisma (*Tos. Temur.*, IV, 10) who was a disciple of R. Gamaliel II (*Sifrê Deut.*, 16; *Horaj.*, 10 a, b) and discussed a question with R. Meir, R. Jehudah, and R. Josê (*'Arakh.*, II, 4) after the year 136, so that there appears to be no foundation for Weiss's view (II, 121) that R. Ḥaninah lived before the year 70. On the other hand, as he died in the times of R. Jehudah and R. Josê (*Bekhor.*, 30 b), he could have been born before the destruction of the Temple, and if he died very old, could have, as a young priest (*Bekhor.*, 30 b), observed the things reported by him from the Temple; see also Hyman, *Toldoth*, 480 a. In *Jebam.*, XVI, 7, R. Eliezer and R. Joshua tell R. Akiba how once several Levites went to Ṣo'ar, the town of date palm-trees; on the way one of them was taken ill and brought to the nearest inn. On their way back they learnt from the female innkeeper that their companion had died and she had buried him, and on her evidence the rabbis allowed the widow to re-marry. This seems to have happened in the times of the rabbis mentioned, so that the Levites as their contemporaries would also have survived the destruction of Jerusalem.

[2] Aptowitzer in *MGWJ*, LII, 1908, 744 ff.

b. Bethera gave evidence about the marriage of a eunuch in Jerusalem.[1] Naḥum the Mede was, according to R. Nathan (*Tos. B. bath.*, IX, 1, *Kethub.*, 105 a), a judge in Jerusalem; Nazirites who had come from Babylonia to Jerusalem to fulfil their vow, but found the Temple destroyed, he directed as to their duties (*Nazir*, V, 4), and a few statements of his show him a teacher in Judaea after the year 70. R. Dosa b. Harkinas, a member of the school in Jamnia, was old and blind when the discussions between the schools of the Shammaiites and Hillelites were being settled in Jamnia; he must, therefore, have been born long before the destruction of Jerusalem. He remembered how Joshua b. Ḥananjah—born at the latest in the year 50—had been carried in his cradle by his mother to a school in order to accustom his ears early to the Torah (*jer. Jebam.*, I, 3 a, 72, b. 16 a), and he was a contemporary of R. Joḥanan b. Zakkai and of R. Ḥaninah, the vice high priest (*Kethub.*, XIII, 1, *Neg.*, I, 4). Ḥizkijah אבי עקש, not otherwise known, gave evidence before R. Gamaliel II in the name of Gamaliel I (*Bekhor.*, 38 a, *Sifra*, 53 d), so that he must have been born about the year 40. R. Gamaliel II himself, the son of Simeon b. Gamaliel the opponent of Josephus during the revolution (*Vita*, 38) and president of the Synedrion, was saved from the punishing hands of the Romans by R. Joḥanan b. Zakkai (*Gitt.*, 56 b) whom he later succeeded in the presidency of the beth-din in Jamnia. He remembered how his father counteracted as to a law of the Sabbath the interfering presence of a Sadducee living with him in the same lane (*'Erub.*, VI, 2), and how he left the prescribed corner on fruit-trees (*Pe'ah*, II, 4) and what kind of bread was not baked in his father's house on a holy day (*Beṣah*, II, 6). From all this it is evident that he was at least a man of 20 at the death of his father. His co-president in Jamnia, R. Eleazar b. 'Azarjah, was a priest and probably quite young in

[1] *Jebam.*, VIII, 4; see Brüll, *Einleitung*, I, 30.

the year 70, as R. Dosa b. Harkinas, though knowing his father, did not know him (*Jebam.*, 16 a); R. Akiba speaks of him as descended of great men and in the tenth generation from Ezra (*jer. Berakh.*, IV, 7d, 10, b. 27b). Also 'Elisha b. 'Abuja must have escaped young from Jerusalem where his father was a wealthy man; R. Joshua and R. Eliezer, the disciples of R. Joḥanan b. Zakkai, attended his circumcision in Jerusalem (*jer. Ḥagigah*, II, 77 b, 38). Many years after the destruction he attended R. Akiba's school, and during and after the Hadrianic religious persecutions he lived in Tiberias, where he died about the year 140.[1] A R. Jehudah b. Gadish, not otherwise known, testified before R. Eliezer that his father's household bought in Jerusalem fish-brine for the equivalent of the second tithe.[2]

Incidentally women, who survived the catastrophe of the year 70, are also mentioned in the Talmud. R. Eleazar b. Ṣadok saw Martha, the daughter of Boethos and the wife of the high priest Joshua b. Gamala, tied by her hair to the tail of a horse and dragged from Jerusalem to Lydda.[3] R. Joḥanan b. Zakkai saw the daughter of Nakdimon b. Gorjon, one of the wealthiest men in Jerusalem, in Ma'on in abject poverty.[4] There are references to R. Tarfon's mother (*jer. Kiddush.*, IV, 61 b, 18, b. 31 b) and his sister whose children he taught (*Zebaḥ.*, 62 b) and also to R. Ishmael's

[1] *Jer. Ḥag.*, II, 77 c.

[2] *'Erub.*, 27 a, bottom; *Tos. Ma'as. sheni*, I, 14. His father came only on pilgrimage to Jerusalem, as no man of the capital was allowed to redeem the tithe; but *Tos.* has, 'was selling,' so that the man lived in Jerusalem (see Schwarz, *Tosifta*, I, 174 a). We find that the Galilean R. Josê, after the year 136, met Abba Eleazar, who told him how he had sacrificed in Jerusalem (*Ḥag.*, 16 b), and that R. Josê could have received information about the Temple and Jerusalem from his father Ḥalaftha, who had seen even R. Gamaliel I on the Temple mount (*Tos. Sabb.*, XIII, 2, and parallels). Those and other scholars who lived in Galilee are not discussed here.

[3] *Midrash Threni*, I, 16, *jer. Kethub.*, V, 30 b, c, *Gitt.*, 56 a; Bacher, *Tannaiten*, I, 47, 6.

[4] *Sifrê Deut.*, 305; *Kethub.*, 66 b; *Mekhiltha* on Exod. xix. 1, 61 a.

mother (*Niddah*, 48 b, *Tos.*, VI, 8), R. Eliezer's mother (*jer. Jebam.*, III, 13 c, 60) and his wife, the sister of R. Gamaliel (*B. meṣ.*, 59 b). Naturally many thousands of men and women, nowhere referred to specially, were saved and remained in Judaea. There was no occasion for mentioning them, though general references are not wanting. It is also worth stating that some of the so-called Nathins survived the destruction of Jerusalem, for in the times of R. Eleazar b. ʿAzarjah it was proposed to recognize them as proper Israelites.[1]

5. By tracing some places in Judaea in which, after the destruction of Jerusalem, Jews lived in greater or smaller numbers, a clearer and more complete view of actual conditions in the country can be obtained. Of Jerusalem, strange to say, very little is known from the Talmudic literature. It is true, some scholars state that soon after the catastrophe some Jewish and Christian families returned to Jerusalem, preferring to live in poor houses among the ruins of the holy city to cities in Judaea,[2] but no Jewish source is adduced, nor is such known to me. Only Eusebius (*Hist. eccl.*, IV, 5 ff., V, 12) reports that the Christians, who during the siege of Jerusalem had fled to Pella, soon returned. And Epiphanius, just as reliable a historian as Eusebius, relates (*De mensuris*, § 14) that, when visiting Jerusalem (130–1), Hadrian found the city and the Temple destroyed and only a few houses inhabited and a small church.[3] R. Simeon b. Eleazar of the second half of the second century reports (*Semaḥ.*, X) that R. Gamaliel II had in Jamnia a hired grave for the temporary burial of members of his family whence they were later taken to Jerusalem. Whether other noble families continued in the same way burying their dead in their family

[1] *Jer. Kiddush.*, IV, 65 c, 59; in *b. Jebam.*, 79 b, top, Rabbi is mentioned instead, evidently the name Eleazar having fallen out.

[2] See, for instance, Munk, *Palestine*, 604 b; Besant-Palmer, *Jerusalem*, 52, and others.

[3] See Herzog-Hauck, *RE*, VIII, 687 ff.

graves in Jerusalem, is not reported, but it is not improbable. The ruins of the Temple were visited by scholars, as R. Gamaliel II, R. Eleazar b. 'Azarjah, R. Joshua, and R. Akiba (*Makk.*, 24 b), who were grieved by seeing a fox coming out from the ruins of the Holy of Holies. R. Josê also entered one of the ruins of Jerusalem to pray (*Berakh.*, 3 a); and 'Elisha b. 'Abuja told R. Meir that he once on a Day of Atonement that fell on the Sabbath, rode by the Holy of Holies and heard a heavenly voice inviting him to repentance (*jer. Ḥag.*, II, 77 b, 59, *Kohel. r.*, 7, 8). As he was then a sinner, it occurred about the years 120–135.

There is even some, though late, evidence that scholars and other Jews visited Jerusalem on the festivals. R. Shela of Kefar-Thamartha, between 280–300, states (*Cant. r.*, 8, 9, 3): though the Temple is destroyed, the Israelites have not stopped their pilgrimages three times a year. In *Threni r.*, 1, 17, a number of differences between the present and the old pilgrimage are stated; and R. Berekhjah of the fourth century points out that both the going up and the return are very quiet, according to R. Levi of about the year 300 both are done secretly. In a Baraitha, *Nedar.*, 23a, a man prohibited his wife by a vow to go on pilgrimage; when she still went up, the husband asked R. Josê's advice. It is true the destination is not stated, but it is hardly doubtful that Jerusalem and not Jamnia is meant.[1] R. Eleazar b. Shammu'a, in the middle of the second century, took to his house a shipwrecked Roman when the Jews went on pilgrimage to Jerusalem (*Kohel. r.*, 11, 1). R. Ḥaninah, R. Jonathan, and R. Joshua b. Levi, about the year 250, on their way to Jerusalem bought some produce and wanted to redeem it outside Jerusalem, but an old man reminded them: your fathers did not proceed in that way, but declared such produce free property and redeemed it (*jer. Ma'as.*

[1] See the pilgrimages of people of Asia to Jamnia in *Tos. Ḥull.*, III, 10; *Parah*, VII, 4; *Mikw.*, IV, 6.

sh., III, 54 b, 20). Though the report is far from being clear, it is evident that the law concerning the second tithe in its relation to Jerusalem was still observed. Accordingly R. Eliezer b. Hyrkanos, about the year 100, declared the fruit of the fourth year of his vineyard free property and expected the poor who would take possession of it, to take it to Jerusalem (*Rosh haShan.*, 31 b). And R. Akiba changed for R. Gamaliel and R. Joshua the money of redemption of their second tithe[1] to spend it in Jerusalem.[2] R. Jonathan was another time on his way to Jerusalem to pray there,[3] and fifty years before, about the year 200, R. Ishmael b. R. Josê went up to Jerusalem to pray (*Genes. r.*, 81, 3; *jer.* *'AZ*, V, 44 d, 41). In spite of the statements of the church fathers that the Jews were not allowed to visit Jerusalem, except on the 9th of 'Ab, they seem to have gone up regularly on various occasions, so that R. Joḥanan, between 250 and 279, was able to say that the city was open to everybody: whoever likes at present to go up, goes up, but in the future only invited people will go up to Jerusalem (*B. bathra*, 75 b, top). R. Joḥanan b. Marja in the name of R. Pinḥas says (*jer. Pesaḥ.*, VII, 35 b, 39): we see the scholars take off their shoes under the doorstep of the Temple mount[4]; and in *Threni r.*, 1, 17, Vespasian places guards 18 miles from Poma'im, who inquired of the pilgrims whom they recognized as their lord. All these

[1] *Ma'as. sh.*, II, 7; it naturally seems more probable to refer it to the time of the Temple, but then R. Gamaliel II lived in Jerusalem and had there no occasion for redeeming that tithe. And when R. Joshua and R. Gamaliel knew R. Akiba, it was long after the year 70; for all attempts to place Akiba's time of study before that year seem futile.

[2] R. Eleazar b. 'Azarjah is in *Sabb.*, 54 b, *Beṣah*, 23 a, said to have given thousands of calves as tithe. This, however, had to be offered as peace-offering, and was, according to *Bekhor.*, 53 a, not to be given after the destruction of the Temple; see *Tosafoth* to all the passages. On the other hand, the *Mishnah Bekhor.*, IX, 1, states that it had to be given, but not what should be done with the tithe from cattle.

[3] *Genes. r.*, 32, 10, *Cant. r.*, 4, 4, *Deut. r.*, III, 6, 7, 14.

[4] See Lewy in *haMaggid*, 1870, 149 b, top.

reports agree in referring to a free pilgrimage to Jerusalem.

6. Lydda and Jamnia, we have seen, were populated in the year 68 by Vespasian with a suitable number of loyal Jews (*Wars*, IV, 8, 1). They were in no way interfered with by the Romans or the national Jews during the revolution of the years 69 and 70. Whether those Jews went up to Jerusalem to celebrate the Passover in April 70 and were there surprised by the Roman siege, is not reported; but as they had previously surrendered to the Romans, and Jerusalem was in the hands of the revolutionists, a pilgrimage of those Jews is not probable. Besides, as the Roman army began the siege of Jerusalem on the 14th of Nissan, after one of the legions, the fifth, had marched from Caesarea by Emmaus to Jerusalem, it must have passed through or near Lydda at the latest on the 12th of Nissan, and thus prevented the possible pilgrimage of any inhabitants of Lydda or Jamnia which were at a day's distance from Jerusalem. In any case, both these towns had organized Jewish communities, and we can easily understand why R. Joḥanan b. Zakkai asked Titus's or Vespasian's permission to settle just in Jamnia; and even the statement that he asked for the scholars of Jamnia (*Gitt.*, 56 b) could be literally true, as there may have been scholars among the settlers. Jamnia became the seat of the great school and the beth-din of R. Joḥanan, which is often described as a meeting in the vineyard of Jamnia.[1] Lydda had several schools, in one of which the teachers met to decide questions, and before this meeting R. Tarfon placed a practical case (*Beṣah*, III, 5)[2]; five members constituted the body.[3] R. Eliezer, who is pointed out as the authority in Lydda

[1] Krauss in I. Lewy's *Festschrift*, 21 ff.

[2] Cf. R. Jehudah's report in *'Erub.*, IV, 4, and *jer.*, IV, 22 a, with *Baraitha b. 'Erub.*, 45 a: R. Tarfon entered on a Sabbath morning the school and taught all day.

[3] *Jer. Beṣah*, III, 62 a, 55; see my *'Am ha'areṣ*, p. 302, 5.

(*Synh.*, 32 b), had a school of his own, called the great[1]; it looked like a racecourse, and there sitting on a stone R. Eliezer taught (*Cant. r.*, 1, 3, 1). There were also several synagogues in Lydda, some of which were built by the ancestors of R. Ḥama b. Ḥaninah (*jer. Shekal.*, V, 49 b, 33), one was of the טרסיים.[2] A school for children is mentioned in the time of R. Akiba in *Semaḥ.*, II, 4. Beside Alexa, a man of importance and generally esteemed (*Tos. Ḥag.*, II, 13), and the family of a Menaḥem (*Synh.*, 33 a) whose property will have to be referred to later, the family of Nithzah is mentioned, with whom R. Tarfon and his disciples stayed on a Sabbath[3]; and the family of 'Aris in whose upper chamber the question heavy with consequences was decided by a meeting of teachers, whether in religious persecutions a Jew has to sacrifice his life for any religious commandment (*Kiddush.*, 40 b, *Sifrê Deut.*, 41). A man Gornos, whose little son committed suicide because the father threatened to punish him (*Semaḥ.*, II, 4), is in the first century interesting for his name. The same applies to a doctor Theodos, who in the presence of R. Akiba and other teachers, examined human bones in the synagogue of Tarsijim mentioned above (*Nazir*, 52 a, and parallels). In the bakers' hall (in the market of Lydda) R. Eliezer was found by R. Josê b. Darmaskith.[4] The vendors of Lydda rejoiced when R. Tarfon fixed the amount of overreaching, justifying a buyer to return the article, at one-eighth of the value; but when he added that the buyer may retract the whole day of the transaction,

[1] *Mekhiltha*, 53 b; *R. Simeon*, p. 82; *Bekhor.*, 5 b; *RÉJ*, 1910, LX, 107 ff.

[2] *Nazir*, 52 a; the parallels in *Tos. 'Ahil.*, IV, 2, *jer. Berakh.*, I, 3 a, 19, do not give the name.

[3] *Sabb.*, 29 b; *Tos.*, II, 5; cf. *Tos. 'Erub.*, IX, 2.

[4] *Tos. Jadaj.*, II, 16. In *Tos. 'Ahil.*, XVIII, 18, about the year 200 Rabbi, R. Ishmael b. R. Josê and R. Eliezer haKappar stayed for the Sabbath in the food-shop of Pazzi in Lydda, and R. Pinḥas b. Jair, who lived in Lydda, sat in front of them discussing with them halachic questions.

they reverted to the accepted rule of the earlier rabbis, for they sold dear.[1] Strange to say, very few details are mentioned of the life of the Jews in Jamnia, though sometimes 72 members of the school were at the same time present in the town (*Zebaḥ.*, I, 3) and even 85 (*Tos. Kelim*, 3 II, 4). Only the family of a ben-Zaza is mentioned, for whose mother R. Gamaliel held a great public mourning (*Rosh haShan.*, 25 a), and the bath of a certain Diskos used for levitically purifying vessels, which was once the subject of a discussion between R. Tarfon and R. Akiba.[2]

7. Around Lydda and Jamnia as centres several smaller places had Jewish inhabitants. When a certain Alexa died in Lydda, the men of the villages came to bewail him, but R. Tarfon prohibited the public mourning owing to the holy day.[3] In one of those villages, east of Lydda, Kefar-Tabi, R. Eliezer of Lydda had a vineyard[4]; another was Kefar-Luddim (*Gitt.*, I, 1) west of Lydda, already outside Palestine, although quite close to Lydda (*Gitt.*, 4 a). R. Akiba had his school in benê-Berak,[5] a very fertile

[1] *B. meṣ.*, IV, 3; they are mentioned also in *Tos. Pesaḥ.*, X, 10, but see b. 116 a.

[2] *Kiddush.*, 66 b; *jer. Terum.*, VIII, 45 b, 36; *Tos. Mikw.*, I, 17.

[3] *Tos. Ḥag.*, II, 13; in *Rosh haShan.*, 29 b, on the day of a New Year which fell on the Sabbath, all the towns had assembled in Jamnia around R. Joḥanan b. Zakkai. The Munich MS. and other authorities in Rabbinowicz, however, have only, 'and all had assembled.' In *Rosh haShan.*, I, 6, it is reported: once over forty pairs of witnesses who had observed the appearance of the new moon, passed on their way to the beth-din in Jamnia through Lydda, where R. Akiba stopped them from proceeding; R. Gamaliel blamed him for it. In the parallel *Baraitha*, 22 a, top, *jer.*, I, 57 b, 70, R. Jehudah says that R. Akiba would not have committed such a mistake, but that it was Shazpar, the head of Gadar, who did it and who was for it deposed by R. Gamaliel. The incident shows how many men in the neighbourhood of Lydda were ready to go and give such evidence.

[4] *Rosh haShan.*, 31 b; it is again mentioned in *Tos. 'Ahil.*, IV, 2, *jer. Berakh.*, I, 3 a, 18, *Nazir*, 52 a: R. Jehudah said: boxes containing human bones were brought from Kefar-Tabi to a synagogue in Lydda.

[5] *Synh.*, 32 b, and *Pesaḥ-Haggadah*; in *Tos. Sabb.*, III, 3, b. 40 a, R. Jehudah reports that R. Akiba and R. Eleazar b. 'Azarjah bathed in a bath in benê-

district near Joppé, R. Joshua b. Ḥananjah taught in Peḳi'in between Lydda and Jamnia,[1] R. Ishmael in Kefar-'Aziz,[2] his teacher Neḥunjah b. Hakanah is once called a man of Emmaus[3] where R. Joshua visited him. This town had a cattle-market in which R. Gamaliel of Jamnia, accompanied by R. Joshua and R. Akiba, bought cattle for the wedding-feast of his son[4]; it was Amwâs in the Shefelah at the entrance into the mountains and reached from Jamnia by the valley of Surar.[5] Owing to its strategical importance it probably had a Roman garrison. R. Eleazar b. 'Arakh, the favourite disciple

Berak; see also *Synh.*, 96 b, and Rabbinowicz. R. Akiba taught also in Lydda, *Semaḥ.*, II, 4, *Nazir*, 52 a.

[1] *Ḥag.*, 3 a, *jer.*, I, 75 d, 54; *Tos. Sotah*, VII, 9; *Synh.*, 32 b. He once went to R. Joḥanan b. Zakkai to berûr-Ḥajil, and the inhabitants of the villages brought them fruit (*Tos. Ma'as.*, II, 1; *jer.*, II, 49 d, 24). R. Joḥanan lived in that place (*Synh.*, 32 b), but it has not been identified yet, nor is there anything to suggest even the district where it was. If the incident refers to a time after the year 70, berûr-Ḥajil must be sought in Judaea in a part inhabited by Jews.

[2] *Kil'aj.*, VI, 4. As R. Joshua visited him there (*Tos.*, IV, 7), it cannot have been far from Peki'in; and as R. Ishmael attended discussions in Jamnia (*Jadaj.*, IV, 3) with other teachers, and on the death of his sons was visited by R. Tarfon, R. Josê the Galilean, R. Eleazar b. 'Azarjah, and R. Akiba (*Moëd k.*, 28 b), he cannot have lived far from Lydda and Jamnia; see Brüll, *Jahrbücher*, I, 41. According to R. Josê (*Kethub.*, V, 8), he lived near Edom, and Neubauer, *Géographie*, 117; *PEF*, Mem., 3, 348 ff.; Buhl, *Geographie*, 163, identify on that Kefar-'Aziz with Ḥirbet 'Aziz not far south of Jutta, but it seems improbable on the evidence adduced. Edom need not mean ancient Idumaea, but the part of Judaea that in Roman times was called Idumaea. In that district beth-Gubrin had Jewish inhabitants, for Jehudah b. Jacob of beth-Gubrin gave evidence with Jacob b. Jiṣḥak of beth-Gufnin concerning Caesarea in *Tos. 'Ahil.*, XVIII, 16. Rabbi declared beth-Gubrin free from priestly dues, *jer. Dammai*, II, 22, c, 55; *JQR*, XIII, 683.

[3] *Midr. Tannaim*, ed. Hoffmann, 175, אמהום with *h* instead of the usual alef, e.g. *jer. Shebi.*, IX, 38 d, 69; see Klein in *RÉJ*, LX, 1910, 106.

[4] *Ḥull.*, 91 b; *Kerith.*, III, 7, 8, here spelled עימאום; Neḥemiah העמסוני is also probably of Emmaus, Grätz in *MGWJ*, II, 1853, 112. Against the identity of the two tells the essential difference of their rules of interpretation, R. Joḥanan reporting כלל ופרט of Neḥunjah in *Shebu.*, 26 a, whereas Neḥemiah applied רבוי ומעוט; *jer. Berakh.*, IX, 14 b, 68, and *Pesaḥ.*, 22 b. Klein thinks that the discussion between R. Neḥunjah and R. Joshua took place in Emmaus, but the report does not suggest it.

[5] G. A. Smith, *Histor. Geography*, 209 ff.

of R. Joḥanan b. Zakkai, after his master's death, settled in Emmaus, a pleasant place with good water.[1] R. Akiba's teacher Naḥum was of Gimzô near Lydda (*Shebu.*, 26 a), R. Eliezer's son Hyrkanos lived in Kefar-'Etam,[2] near Bethlehem, one of R. Joḥanan b. Zakkai's disciples was R. Eleazar of Modeim, a disciple of R. Jehudah b. Baba was Simeon התימני, probably of Thimnah.[3]

In Ma'on in the south of Judaea, several hours' distance from Hebron, R. Joḥanan b. Zakkai saw a Jewish girl picking up grains of barley from the dung of horses (*Mekhil.* on Ex. 19, 1, 61 a); the presence of this teacher with disciples in Ma'on suggests with great probability that Jews lived in the place. Bethlehem seems to have retained its population after the revolution, as is suggested by the well-known legend about the birth of the Messiah (*jer. Berakh.*, II, 5 a; *Threni r.*, 1, 16, 51): an Arab told a Jew, who was working in the field with his cows, that the lowing of his cow announced that Jerusalem had been destroyed, and the lowing of the other cow that the Messiah had been born in birath-'Arabah of beth-Leḥem in Judaea. The Jew left his work and, in order to find the future Messiah, went about selling flannels for children from village to village, from town to town, till he arrived at the village of birath-'Arabah where he found the child. This story assumes that whole

[1] *Kohel. r.*, 7, 7; *Sabb.*, 147 b; *ARN*, XIV, 30 a; 2 *ARN*, XXIX, 30 a; it is not Ḥamtha near Tiberias, but in Judaea, Bacher, *Tann.*, I, 76, 3; by removing from the second version the word Jerusalem all contradictions disappear.

[2] *Jebam.*, XII, 6; but the Mishnah in *jerus. Jebam.* reads Kefar-'Ibdas, the Cambridge Mishnah Kefar-'Akkô.

[3] In *Beṣah*, 21 a; *Tos.*, II, 6; *Mekhiltha R. Simeon*, 17, it is reported: When on one holy day Simeon of Thimnah had not come to the school, R. Jehudah b. Baba asked him the next morning for the reason. Now from *Tos. Berakh.*, IV, 18, we learn that Simeon belonged to R. Tarfon's school in Lydda, and from *Tos. Synh.*, XII, 3, b. 17 b; *B. kam.*, 90 b; Bacher, *Tann.*, I, 444 ff., we see that he had discussions with R. Akiba, as R. Jehudah b. Baba with R. Akiba and R. Jehudah b. Bethera, so that Simeon belonged to the school of Jamnia or Lydda.

districts of Judaea were not destroyed. Reland (*Palaestina*, 647) refers to Anastasius's Biographies of the Roman bishops, where it is reported that St. Euaristus of the times of Domitian and Nerva was the son of a Jew in Bethlehem; later when Hadrian defeated the Jews, he prohibited them to live in the district of Jerusalem and in Bethlehem; this—he says—followed from Tertullian, *Contra Judaeos*, 224, who remarked that in his time no Jew was left in Bethlehem, for none must live in its boundaries.[1] In the *Apocalypse of Baruch*, 47, 1, Baruch goes from the destroyed capital to Hebron to hear there the revelation of God; as the author wrote shortly after the destruction of Jerusalem, he seems to have known that Hebron was still a Jewish town. In Rimmon lived a Jew of means and several priests[2]; the position of the place is not defined, but as R. Jehudah and R. Simeon b. Gamaliel, both scholars of the school of Jamnia, report the incidents, and Rimmon in Judaea is otherwise mentioned,[3] it is probable that this was meant. At the Dead Sea Ṣo'ar was visited by several Levites (p. 12, note 1). Whether the oasis of 'En-gedi, with its balsam plantations administered by representatives of the Roman emperor themselves,[4] had any Jewish inhabitants left, is nowhere reported. But, as only the

[1] See Guérin, *Judée*, I, 202.

[2] *Tos. 'Ahil.*, XVI, 13; *Mikw.*, VI, 2; *Pesaḥ.*, 9 a, *jer.*, I, 28 a, 39.

[3] Zech. xiv. 10; *Tos. Sotah*, XI, 14; S. Klein, *Beiträge z. Geographie*, 94, 3, thinks of Rimmon in Joshua xix. 13, but the two teachers report, as in many other instances, Judaean experiences. R. Simeon b. Joḥai in the lifetime of his teacher R. Akiba stayed for the Sabbath in Kefar-beth-Fagi (*Tos. Me'ilah*, I, 5, b. 7 a), where he met another disciple of R. Akiba. As it was on his way from Judaea to Galilee, the position is difficult to define.

[4] Pliny, *H. N.*, V, 15; Galerius, vol. XIV, p. 25, Kühn; cf. Hölscher, *Palaestina in d. pers. u. hellen. Zeit*, 49. In *Midr. Cant.*, ed. Grünhut, to i. 14, it is said that 'En-gedi was beautiful, and wine was made there in levitical purity for libations in the Temple; and R. Josef the Babylonian from a Baraitha states in *Sabb.*, 26 a, that balsam was gathered in from 'En-gedi to Ramatha. The vineyards there bore four times a year fruit (*Agad. Cant.* on i. 14).

sicarii had during the revolution driven out the inhabitants (*Wars*, IV, 7, 2) and only the children and women, about 700 were killed, it is very probable that the men returned after the war to 'En-gedi. Eusebius (*Onom.*, *s.v.*) indeed says that the place was in his time a very large Jewish town.

In Jericho R. Gamaliel with other rabbis stayed on some occasion (*Tos. Berakh.*, IV, 15, b. 37 a) which suggests a Jewish community there. As it was not destroyed by the Romans in the revolution and only a part of its population perished by the sword, while the greater part escaped into the mountains opposite Jerusalem (*Wars*, IV, 8, 2), many may have afterwards returned, or Jewish deserters loyal to the Romans may have been settled there under the protection of the garrison and the fortified camp (IV, 9, 1). Interesting evidence proves that Ḥadid and 'Onô in the north-west of Judaea had Jewish inhabitants after the year 70. R. Joshua and R. Jakim of Ḥadid[1] gave evidence (before the authorities in Jamnia) about a point of religious law. Ḥananjah of 'Onô obtained a ruling from R. Akiba when the latter was kept by the Romans in prison, and brought it before rabbis, among whom was R. Josê.[2] Further north, beyond benê-Berak, Kefar-Saba,

[1] *'Eduj.*, VII, 5, reads Hadar, but the Cambridge and Naples *Mishnah* and other texts quoted by Rabbinowicz have Ḥadid, the place mentioned in Ezra ii. 33; Neh. vii. 37, xi. 35; 1 Chron. viii. 12, as Adida in 1 Macc. xii. 38, xiii. 13; in the Bible passages together with Lydda and 'Onô, as they were neighbours, similarly in *'Arakh.*, IX, 6, b. 32 a, Ḥadid and 'Onô in Judaea as fortified since ancient times. In *Kethub.*, 111 b, bottom, R. Jacob b. Dosithai says that he walked from Lydda to 'Onô to his ankles in fig honey.

[2] *Gitt.*, VI, 7. In *Tos. Synh.*, II, 13, b. 11 b, *jer.*, I, 18 d, 76, he testifies that the intercalation of a year may take place only in Judaea, exceptionally also in Galilee. It is obvious that that evidence was taken when owing to the Hadrianic persecutions the religious life of the Jewish community had to be guided from Galilee. Therefore the words 'before R. Gamaliel' in *Tos.* are a mistake. In *Sifrê zutta* on Num. xv. 4 in *Jalkut*, Num. 746, *Horovitz*, 92, a R. Papias of 'Onô is mentioned; whether he is identical with R. Papias, a colleague of R. Akiba, is uncertain. About the year 200 R. Simai and R. Ṣadok went to Lydda to intercalate the

which may be identical with Antipatris, had Jewish inhabitants. For R. Meir reports (*Tos. Niddah*, VIII, 5): a dead human body was suspected to have been buried under a certain sycamore in Kefar-Saba, but nothing was found.[1] A similar case is reported from beth-Ḥoron, south-east of Modeim, by R. Joshua, viz. that dead bodies were suspected in a rock.[2] Gofna, a town north of

year and, when staying for the Sabbath in 'Onô, gave a decision on religious law (*Ḥull.*, 56 b). R. 'Aibo of the fourth century says (*Cant. r.*, 2, 2; *Lev. r.*, 23, 5; *Threni r.*, 1, 17): God ordered Jacob's enemies to surround him, so Ḥalamish surrounds Naweh, Castra Ḥaifa, Susitha Tiberias, Jericho No'aran, and Lydda 'Onô. As 'Onô is mentioned as an old fortress, we would suggest 'Onô to Lydda, but Lydda rose in importance and may have superseded 'Onô even as fortress or merely as city (*JQR*, XIII, 733). In *jer. Gitt.*, IV, 46 a, 36, R. 'Ammi ruled that if a slave escaped from abroad and reached 'Oni, he must not be surrendered to his master (for the place is in Palestine), if to 'Antris, he may be surrendered (for it is not in Palestine), if to 'Aparkoris, it is doubtful. 'Antaris cannot be Antarados, as Krauss, *Lehnwörter*, II, 72, suggests, for the place must be on the border of Palestine. Where is 'Oni? Is it identical with 'Onô, and are the other two places in Philistia? Another place is mentioned in *jer. Synh.*, I, 18 c, 71: 'we still find that the year was solemnly initiated in Ba'alath (in Judaea). This was at times reckoned to Judah, sometimes to Dan. But do we not find that the year was initiated in Balath? Here the houses stood in Judah, the fields lay in Dan.' In the two places mentioned the ceremony of initiating the new year was performed after the authoritative beth-din had long been transferred to Galilee. We learn that there were Jews in those places in the fourth century, though it may confidently be assumed that the same applied to earlier times, as Ba'alath was last in the line Lydda—Modeim—Ba'alath (see, however, Neubauer, 99 ff.). The same may apply to 'Ekron, of which Eusebius says that it was east of Jamnia between this and Azotus and a great Jewish village.

[1] It is again mentioned in *jer. Dammai*, II, 22 c, 47: the law of Dammai applies to Samaritans in Pondaka of 'Ammuda and of Tibatha to Kefar-Saba; see Schürer, II, 156 ff. Antipatris seems to have been raised at some time or other in character as town, for *Threni r.*, 1, 5; ed. *Buber*, 33 a, says: You find that before the destruction of Jerusalem no city was in their sight of value, but after the destruction Caesarea became a metropolis, Antipatris a central town, and Neapolis a colony. As the latter became a colony only under Philip Arabs, the statement was made at the earliest in the year 250; yet Antipatris may have been distinguished at a much earlier time.

[2] *Tos. Niddah*, VIII, 7; in the parallel *Baraitha Niddah*, 61 a, the informant is Abba Saul, and the scholar who suggested a new method of examining the rock was R. Joshua.

Jerusalem, was conquered and spared by Vespasian (*Wars*, IV, 9, 9; VI, 2, 2), and Titus sent there the nobles who had deserted to him from Jerusalem, to stay there till the war would be finished (VI, 2, 2, 3). Whether in addition to the original inhabitants of the town, mostly priests (*Berakh.*, 44 a; *jer. Ta'an.*, IV, 69 a, 57), any of the nobles of Jerusalem settled there, is not known.

Another place of interest is Adasa, of which R. Jehudah in a Baraitha (*'Erub.*, 60 a) reports: There was a village in Judaea called Ḥadashah where there were 50 inhabitants, men, women, and children, and being an annexe itself, the rabbis measured by it annexes of towns (*'Erub.*, V, 6). It seems hardly doubtful that R. Jehudah, as in his many other reports, referred to Judaea of his own times before the bar-Kochba war. Now Adasa is known from 1 Macc. vii. 40, 45, and was, according to Josephus (*Antiq.*, XI, 10, 5), 30 stadia from beth-Ḥoron, probably identical with Adasa near Gofna.[1] But as R. Jehudah says that Ḥadashah was in Judaea and *jer. 'Erub.*, V, 22 d, 54, quotes to it Joshua xv. 37, it must have been the one nearer Jerusalem, and was the small suburb of an unnamed Jewish town before the year 135. In *'Eduj.*, VI, 2, 3, R. Joshua gave evidence with R. Neḥunjah b. 'Elinathan of Kefar-haBabli, obviously in Jamnia as also evident from R. Neḥunjah's discussions with R. Eliezer. His native place occurs again in *'Abôth*, IV, 20, as that of R. Josê b. Jehudah, who is identified with Josê or 'Isi the Babylonian.[2] In a *Baraitha Pesaḥ.*, 113 b, he is further identified with Josê of Huṣal; and as there is a place Huṣal of the Babylonians in Benjamin mentioned in *Kethub.*, 111 a; *Megil.*, 5 b, the matter seems quite clear.[3] There was then a village

[1] Eusebius, p. 220; Schürer, *Geschichte*, I, 218, 28.

[2] *Jer. B. kam.*, III, 3 d, 37; Bacher, *Tann.*, II, 371, 3.

[3] In *Nedar*, 81 a, a statement of Isi b. Jehudah is identical with that of Jehudah of Huṣa (see Ratner on *Shebi'ith*, VIII, 38 b, 10, p. 77); see also *Kiddush.*, 58 b, top, and Derenbourg, *Essai*, 483.

Huṣal in the territory of Benjamin, a Babylonian colony, about the year 150, which, however, must have existed earlier. In addition to these places where Jewish inhabitants can only be inferred, there are a few in connexion with which Jews are expressly mentioned, but their geographical position can only be suggested. R. Jehudah reports[1] that about the levitical purity of some pots in Kefar-Signa a dispute arose between R. Gamaliel and other scholars; and R. Eliezer reports that a fire broke out on the threshing-floor of the same place and a doubt arose about the separation of priestly dues.[2] It was then a Jewish place that had survived the destruction of Jerusalem. R. Josê reports that from Kefar-'Iddim a case concerning more than 60 troughs was brought before R. Gamaliel to define their levitical quality (*Tos. Kelim*, 2, XI, 2). As R. Gamaliel measured the vessels, they had been all brought to Jamnia, and the place cannot have been very far from that town; its inhabitants were either priests or trough-makers.[3]

8. A characteristic instance of a town that survived unimpaired the catastrophe of the year 70 is Betthar, the last fortress of bar-Kochba. R. Josê says in a Baraitha: Betthar continued for 52 years after the destruction of the Temple and then it perished, because it had lighted lamps (of joy) at the destruction.[4] And R. Simeon b. Gamaliel reports: There were in Betthar 500 schools for children, and the smallest of them had not less than 500

[1] *Tos. Kelim*, 1, IV, 4, variants in *MGWJ*, 1901, XLV, 22.

[2] *Tos. Terum.*, III, 18; from the same place wine was in Temple times taken for sacrifices, *Menaḥ.*, VIII, 6. Neubauer, 84, suggests Sukneh near Joppé, but the statement that Kefar-Signa was in the valley is too vague for definition.

[3] In *Tos. Ḥull.*, III, 23, b. 62 a, the opponents of R. Eliezer refer to the fact that the people of Kefar-Thamartha in Judaea ate a certain fowl as permitted, because it had a crop, a sign of purity. They were Jews; but it is not clear whether this refers to our period after the year 70.

[4] *Jer. Ta'an.*, IV, 69 a, 23; *Threni r.*, 2, 2. In *Seder 'Olam*, XXX, it says: From Vespasian's war to that of Quietus were 52 years; see Ratner, p. 73 b, note 78; Schürer, *Geschichte*, I, 696, note.

children.[1] It had bouleutai (*jer. Ta'an.*, IV, 69 a, 26), and a beth-din as Jamnia (*Synh.*, 17 b), and was consequently a town of importance. Add to this the full report of Dio Cassius, LXIX, 14, that the Roman general, Julius Severus, sent by Hadrian to Judaea against the Jewish rebels under bar-Kochba, razed fifty of their best fortresses and 985 of their most important villages, and that 580,000 men were killed in the sorties and battles, and the number of those who perished by famine, disease, and fire, could not be defined, so that almost the whole of Judaea became a desert, as it had been predicted before the war. Even granted that Dio grossly exaggerated the feat of the Roman general, it will have to be admitted that Judaea was fairly populated, as many thousands of those who had been driven from their towns and villages by the approach of the Roman armies in the years 66–70, after the restoration of peace gradually returned to their homes or settled in other places of Judaea that had been depopulated. Just as Betthar, there must have been several towns of greater or less importance. For in the report about R. Akiba's execution in the Hadrianic persecutions it is stated in rather obscure terms: within twelve months after this בולאות in Judaea ceased. These were cities of importance of which there were at some time at least 24.[2] But apart

[1] In the parallel in *B. kam.*, 83 a, R. Simeon b. Gamaliel says that in his father's house (school) were a thousand children, 500 learnt Torah and 500 Greek science, and of all only he and his cousin in Asia remained. Betthar is not mentioned, but apparently Jamnia is meant.

[2] *Semaḥ.*, VIII: מכאן ועד שנים עשר חדש פסקו בולאות שביהודה שנאמר חרדו שאננות רגזה בוטחות, שאננות אלו בולאות שביהודה, בוטחות אלו קרקסיאות, לא היה בו לשון בוטחות אלא טרכסין. Two groups of places are referred to: one בולאות, the other קרקסיאות, for which ס׳ חסידים, 80, 1, reads חרדו שאננות אלו טרקסיאות. The verb פסק without complementary verb can hardly refer to persons, but only to inanimate things, best to cities that felt too secure, open places as opposed to fortified towns that offered safety, as already N. Brüll in his *Jahrbücher*, I, 41, 89, explained them. As כרקום means a fortress in *T. Jebam.*, XIV, 8: fortress of Betthar, קרקסיאות, is most probably a corruption of that word. As to the meaning of בולאות, a Baraitha cited by R. Josef in *Gitt.*, 37 a, top, reads: I shall break the pride of your

from this the material, collected above about existing cities and villages inhabited by Jews, conclusively proves that Judaea was still fairly populated after the year 70.

II. Economic Conditions and Landed Property.

1. From Josephus we have derived the information that in the course of the long war in Judaea between the years 66 and 70, several towns and villages surrendered to the Romans, and that the Jewish inhabitants probably retained their property and all their possessions. In some other places loyal Jews were settled, and they must have either received from the Romans or leased fields from Vespasian and Titus. To many of the nobles who had deserted from Jerusalem into the Roman camp, Titus promised to restore their property after the war. Though the redemption of the promise is nowhere reported, Josephus's case is an instance of it, for his fields near Jerusalem were restored to him, and when they were required for the Roman garrison, Titus gave Josephus other property in the plain (*Vita*, 76). On the other hand we are told (*Wars*, VII, 6, 6) that Vespasian declared the land of

might (Lev. xxvi. 19), these are the בולאות in Judaea (not to be identified with the interpretation of the same verse in *Sifra*, 111 d, § 2: These are the nobles who are the pride of Israel, as Pappos b. Jehudah and Lulianus, Alexandri and his companions, for the characteristic word is not there, see Bacher, *Tann.*, I, 52, 6). And in *jer. Nedar.*, III, 38 a, 13, *Pesiktha r.*, XXII, 112 b ff., R. Samuel b. Naḥman says: Twenty-four בוליות were in the Darom and all were destroyed owing to a useless, though true oath. Here it is evident from the word חרבו that buildings or towns are meant. R. Ḥaninaḥ, the vice high-priest, says in *'Abôth R. Nathan*, XX, 36 b: The sons of my mother were angry with me (Cant. i. 6), refer to בולאות in Judaea, who shook off the yoke of God and set over them a human king. Here either leading men of the country are referred to or the elders in 1 Sam. viii. 4 who committed that mistake; as R. Ḥaninah hardly knew bar-Kochba, and, as far as we know, in the year 116 no king of Judaea was elected, the reference is still obscure. If he meant towns with proper constitutions, he may have referred to the revolution in the years 66–70, though we only know of Menaḥem as a kind of king (Geiger in *ZS*, VIII, 39, and Schlatter, *Zur Topographie*, 121 ff.).

Judaea his private property and disposed of some parts, for instance, by giving to 8,000 veterans fields in Emmaus, near Jerusalem, and by rewarding Josephus. The rest had accordingly to be leased from the emperor, even by the former owners. Before order was restored in this matter, terrible conditions seem to have prevailed in some places of Judaea, as the following incident suggests. One of the wealthiest men of Jerusalem before its destruction,[1] Nakdimon b. Gorjon, most probably perished during the siege of the capital. After the catastrophe his daughter is found by R. Joḥanan b. Zakkai and his disciples starving and picking grains of barley from horses' dung,[2] and, when questioned by the rabbi, explained that the money of her ~~father and her~~ father-in-law was all gone.[3] Such cases of utter impoverishment may have been numerous, while such as continued on their property may also have been many. For Eusebius, in his short account of the bar-Kochba war (*Hist. Eccl.*, IV, 6), says: Tineius Rufus, the governor of Judaea, availing himself of the madness of the rebelling Jews under bar-Kochba, went out against them, killed indiscriminately thousands of men, women, and children, and, according to the law of war, brought the fields of the Jews into his possession.[4]

2. As to details reflecting actual conditions, Josephus offers none, and it is again the Talmud only that contains some very instructive information. Unfortunately this

[1] His wealth and his position are described in *ARN*, XVII, 33 a, VI, 16 a, b; 2 *ARN*, XIII, 16 a; *Kethub.*, 66 b, bottom.

[2] *Sifrê Deut.*, 305, 130 a; *Kethub.*, 66 b; *ARN*, XVII, 33 a; Bacher, *Tannaiten*, I, 42. R. Eleazar b. Ṣadok met her in Akko in abject poverty, *Tos. Kethub.*, V, 10; *jer.*, V, 30 b, 76 ff., b. 67 a.

[3] Josephus in *Wars*, VI, 5, 2, reports that the treasure houses of the Temple were burnt, in which an enormous sum of money, a mass of garments and other precious things, in short, the whole wealth of the Jews was kept, as the wealthy had brought there all their effects.

[4] The same in *jer. Gitt.*, V, 47 b, 11: the enemy decreed persecutions first against Judaea, subdued its people, took their fields and sold them to others.

material is merely incidental and only in very few instances descriptive; in most cases it refers to the time between 80 and 135 in giving illustrative incidents and relating to the observance of the field corner for the poor, the sabbatical year of rest, the priestly dues, and mortgages. When once R. Joshua visited R. Joḥanan b. Zakkai in berûr-Ḥajil, the people of the villages brought them figs (see p. 21, 1); the farmers were Jews and lived in several villages. When R. Eliezer was put in the ban by the school in Jamnia, the world was smitten, one third on the olives, one third on wheat, and one third on barley (*Bar. B. Meṣ.*, 59 b). Evidently Jewish landowners suffered either in the close neighbourhood of Jamnia or in Lydda, where R. Eliezer lived. R. Akiba remarks (*Tos. Pe'ah*, II, 21) that as to the field corner to be left to the poor landowners (בעלי בתים) are liberal.[1] R. Josê relates (*Kil'aj.*, VII, 5) how a man was reported to R. Akiba for sowing seeds in his vineyard in the

---

[1] In 2 *ARN*, XXXI, 34 a, a sentence introduced by הוא היה אומר and attributed to R. Joḥanan b. Zakkai, reads: Force the children (students) away from haughtiness and separate them from בעלי בתים, for these keep people away from the words of the Torah. The wealthy landowners are referred to who not only had no interest in learning, but also dissuaded others from joining the schools. They are identical with the עמי הארץ, to whom R. Dosa b. Harkinas refers in '*Abôth*, III, 10: Sleep in the morning and wine in midday and sitting in the houses of assembly of the 'Ammê ha'areṣ remove man from the world. The comfort described here points to a class of wealthy men. It may be pointed out here that the sentence quoted is in *ARN*, XXI, 37 b explained to refer to those who sit at the corners in the market and divert one from the Torah. The contemporary of R. Joḥanan b. Zakkai, Neḥunjah b. Hakanah, in his prayer in *Baraitha Berakh.*, 28 b, said: I thank Thee God that Thou hast given my lot with those who sit in the school and not with those who sit at the corners; for we both rise early, I for the words of the Torah, they for vain things; I toil and they toil, I receive a reward, they do not; I run to eternal life, they run to hell (in *jer. Berakh.*, IV, 7 d, 39, instead of the corners, theatres and circuses). R. Akiba termed himself an 'Am ha'areṣ in *Pesaḥ.*, 49 b, and in *ARN*, XI, 37 b he said in his later years when a scholar: I thank Thee my God that Thou hast given my lot with those who sit in the school and not with those who sit at the corners in the market. This shows the identity of the latter men with the 'Am ha'areṣ.

sabbatical year; and R. Akiba himself once saw a man prune his vine in the sabbatical year (*jer. Shebi.*, IV, 35 a, 36). The proselyte Akylas, who is found in the company of R. Gamaliel II, R. Eliezer, and R. Joshua,[1] acquired property in Judaea, for his exporting from Judaea to Pontus some produce of the sabbatical year is quoted as a mistake.[2] In benê-Berak, one sold his father's property and died; his relatives protested that he was a minor, and asked R. Akiba to examine his body, but the rabbi refused to have the grave opened (*B. bath.*, 154 a; *Semaḥ.*, IV, 12). A security once signed a bill after the witnesses; when the debt was claimed from him, R. Ishmael ruled that only his movables were liable (*B. bath.*, X, 8). Joshua, R. Akiba's son, married the daughter of a wealthy landowner and agreed with his wife that she should maintain him and allow him to study; when years of drought came, the husband and the wife divided between them her property (*Tos. Kethub.*, IV, 7; *jer.*, V, 29 d, 25). The son of R. Jehudah the baker gave by deed all his property to his wife who was his cousin; when creditors of the husband claimed the property, the rabbis declared the wife's marriage settlement void owing to the gift from the husband, and the property liable for the debt, so that she lost all (*B. bath.*,

[1] He lived in Jamnia, *Tos. Kelim.*, 3, II, 4; *Sabb.*, VII, 18; *Mikw.*, VI, 3; *jer. Meg.*, I, 71 c, 11; *Genes. r.*, 70, 5; *Kohel. r.*, 7, 8; *Num. r.*, 8 end; *Pesik. r.*, XXIII, 117 a.

[2] *Sifra*, 106 c, § 9. When R. Gamaliel died, Akylas burnt more than seventy manehs of money in his honour, *'Abod. z.*, 11 a; *Tos. Sabb.*, VII, 18; *Semaḥ.*, VIII; this shows his wealth. R. Tarfon in Lydda once after the harvest plucked figs from another man's tree, *Nedar.*, 62 a; when the owner of the field found him doing this, he seized him and put him in a sack to drown him. When R. Tarfon sighed and said: Woe to Tarfon, for he will be killed, the man left him and ran away. R. Ḥaninah b. Gamaliel reports that R. Tarfon through all his life could not forgive himself that he had derived this benefit from his position as scholar. The parallel in *jer. Shebi.*, IV, 35 b, 17, reports the incident to have occurred in the sabbatical year, so that the owner of the field was a Jew. As the field-guards who struck R. Tarfon know when hearing the name who R. Tarfon was, they seem Jews.

132 a). R. Joshua once walked across a field by a trodden path; a Jewish girl reproached him for this, and when he pointed as an excuse to the path, she said: Robbers like you trod it (*'Erub.*, 53 b). Once, walking in the road, R. Gamaliel and R. Joshua, owing to the unevenness of the road, walked beside it in the fields. When they noticed R. Pappos b. Jehudah approaching and walking deep in the mud of the road, R. Gamaliel found fault with this self-exhibition; but R. Joshua explained to him who the man was and how blameless his character.[1] The fields to which Jewish law was applied were Jewish property.[2]

The law concerning priestly dues and tithes was observed in spite of changed conditions of property, and as there were many priests in Judaea, among them several scholars, incidents reported about them will throw light on property. R. Tarfon, a priest who survived the destruction of Jerusalem, is termed a very wealthy man (*Nedar.*, 62 a); he owned land and slaves. Once the unusually red face of his disciple, R. Jehudah, attracted his attention. He accounted for it as follows: Thy slaves last night brought us from the field beets and we ate of those without salt; had we taken salt, our faces would look even more red (*Nedar.*, 49 b). R. Tarfon once gave R. Akiba 600 silver centenarii to buy a field, on the income of which they would live; but R. Akiba distributed the money among poor scholars.[3] R. Tarfon

[1] *Jer. Berakh.*, II, 5 d, 5, and *Ratner*, p. 62; in the parallel *B. kam.*, 81 b, the same is told of Jehudah b. Nekosa who was met by Rabbi and R. Ḥijja in Sepphoris about the year 200.

[2] Reference is made to a מציק in Rimmon in *Tos. 'Ahil.*, XVI, 13; *Mikw.*, VI, 2 (see p. 11, 1), who seems to have been a Jew in the service of the Romans, and who, by their assistance, acquired property (*JQR*, XVI, 153). In *Derekh 'ereṣ*, VI, Gaster, מעשיות, 103, a Simeon b. Antipatris received many wayfarers and provided food, drink, and lodging, but striped all visitors who swore by the Torah that they would not eat, but in the end ate. R. Joḥanan b. Zakkai and the teachers, hearing of this, sent R. Joshua b. Ḥananjah to rebuke Simeon. As his place had a bath, it was a town, perhaps Antipatris, as a part of his name.

[3] *Lev. r.*, 34, 16; *Pesik. r.*, XXV, 126 b; in *Kallah* the incident is

received priestly due, Terumah; once an old man met him and asked him why people should speak of him in disparaging terms for his accepting such dues all the year round from anybody, as otherwise all his actions were upright (*Tos. Ḥag.*, III, 36)? R. Tarfon referred to a rule received by him from R. Joḥanan b. Zakkai on which he had based his acceptance of such dues; but he declared, he would henceforth act more strictly. As we learn of his specially solemn dealing with his priestly dues in the days of R. Gamaliel II,[1] it is most probable that also the incident just quoted occurred in Lydda or Jamnia, and not before the year 70 in Jerusalem. In a year of drought he betrothed to himself several women to enable them to eat of his priestly dues.[2] These reports presuppose several Jewish landowners in Lydda who gave from their produce the prescribed dues[3] to R. Tarfon. Probably one of them was R. Simeon Shezuri, whose untithed produce became once accidentally mixed with a

reported differently: R. Tarfon was wealthy, but not liberal. Once R. Akiba suggested to him to buy one or two places (? fields), and R. Tarfon handed to him 4,000 gold denars which R. Akiba distributed among the poor. After that, R. Tarfon gave him more money for distribution. Interesting is his definition of a wealthy man in *Baraitha Sabb.*, 25 b: He who has hundred vineyards, hundred fields and hundred slaves to work them. It shows his standard of wealth and, if the figures are to be taken strictly, also the relation between a unit of field and the number of slaves required for it.

[1] *Sifrê Num.*, 116; *Pesaḥ.*, 72 b; *Sifrê zutta Num.*, 18, 7, *Horovitz*, 112.

[2] *Tos. Kethub.*, V, 1; *jer. Jebam.*, IV, 6 b, 59. In *jer. Kethub.*, V, 29 d, 46, R. Tarfon says that all the food due to a betrothed woman after twelve months should be given to her in the form of priestly due, for such is found everywhere. The parallels do not contain the last sentence; it would imply that there were fields in Jewish possession everywhere.

[3] In a *Baraitha Berakh.*, 35 b, R. Jehudah reports: Earlier generations were different from the present one: those brought in (from the fields) their produce by the way of טרקסימון in order to make the produce liable to tithe; the present generation bring in their produce by the way of courts and enclosures in order to free it from tithe. In the parallel in *jer. Ma'as.*, III, 50 c, 8, R. Jehudah says to Rabbi and R. Josê b. R. Jehudah: See, R. Akiba bought three kinds of produce for one Perutah in order to give tithe of each.

tithed one, and when he asked R. Tarfon what he should do, he advised him to buy produce in the market and to separate from that the required tithe.[1] R. Simeon had, accordingly, fields of his own; the market was supplied by non-Jews, as the context proves, and the Talmud expressly states. Another priest and scholar was R. Eleazar b. ʿAzarjah, a very wealthy man (*Kiddush.*, 49 b), mentioned along with the fabulously rich Eleazar b. Ḥarsom; he who dreams of him, may hope to become rich (*Berakh.*, 57 b). Since he died, the crown of scholars departed, for wealth is their crown (*Sotah*, IX, 15; *jer.* and *b.* end). He gave to R. Josê the Galilean the amount of his wife's marriage settlement to enable him to divorce his wicked wife (*Genes. r.*, 17, 3). No reference is found to R. Eleazar's fields; but as in Rabh's report (*Sabb.*, 54 b) the tithe of his herds were 12,000 calves every year, even taking the figure grossly exaggerated, it presupposes in R. Eleazar's possession either his own or leased pasture lands of great extent.[2] He dealt in wine and oil all his life (*Tos. ʿAbod. z.*, IV, 1; *B. bath.*, 91 a); whether it was his own produce or bought from others, is not indicated. As a priest he used to receive the tithe of the produce of a certain garden till R. Akiba stopped it[3]; the owner

[1] *Tos. Dammai*, V, 22; *jer.*, V, 24 d, 69; *b. Menaḥ.*, 31 a.

[2] A case concerning his cow is specially discussed in *Sabb.*, V, 4; *Beṣah*, II, 8, because he allowed her, against the opinion of the rabbis, to go out on the Sabbath with a strap between her horns. In *jer. Sabb.*, V, 7 c, 28, the rabbis asked R. Eleazar either to leave the school or to stop his cow being let out in that way; see *Ratner* and *Sabb.*, 54 b, bottom. It is evident that the controversy occurred when R. Eleazar was not yet the president of the school in Jamnia.

[3] The garden had two entrances, one in a levitically pure, the other in an unclean place (reported by R. 'Abba in *jer. Maʿas. sheni*, V, 56 b, 71; *b. Jebam.*, 86 b). R. Akiba objected to a priest's taking a tithe which in his opinion was due to Levites only, and he persuaded the owner of the garden to keep the pure entrance shut and, if R. Eleazar should send a disciple for the tithe, to tell him that tithe must be called for by its claimant. R. Eleazar soon found out the author of this trouble, and recognizing his mistake, returned all the tithe which he had ever received.

was a Jew who kept the law about priestly and levitical dues.[1]

3. Several other scholars who had lived before the year 70 in Jerusalem, and now lived with the priests discussed, in Judaea, were possessed of landed property. R. Dosa b. Harkinas (p. 13) was once visited by R. Joshua b. Ḥananjah, R. Eleazar b. 'Azarjah, and R. Akiba (*Jebam.*, 16 a), and he offered them gilded chairs, and his house had several entrances; but of what his wealth otherwise consisted, is not reported, most probably of fields. R. Eliezer was before the year 70 assisting his father, a wealthy farmer in the country, in his work in the field[2]; when, already a married man, he became a disciple of R. Joḥanan b. Zakkai in Jerusalem, and during the siege of Jerusalem followed his master to Jamnia. He lived in Lydda in a house built in Greek style,[3] consisting of at least a room, an upper room, and a dining-room. He had a slave whom he freed when in the synagogue only nine of the requisite ten Israelites were present (*Gitt.*, 38 b),

[1] R. Josê in *Terum.*, IV, 13, reports that a case came before R. Akiba of fifty bundles of vegetables having been accidentally mixed with a bundle, half of which was priestly due. This landowner observed also the rabbinic extension of the duty of tithing to vegetables. A landowning priest was R. Ishmael in Kefar-'Aziz (*Kil'aj.*, VI, 4) who planted vines, figs, and sycamores in his garden, so that he must have otherwise provided for his maintenance (see p. 21, 2). Another priest was Zechariah b. haKaṣṣab, who, with his wife, had escaped from Jerusalem when the Romans took possession of it (*Kethub.*, II, 9, above, p. 10). He assigned to his wife a separate house in his court (*Baraitha Kethub.*, 27, b, bottom; *Tos.*, III, 2; *Semaḥ.*, II), and she lived there. There seems hardly any interval between his escape from Jerusalem and his settling on his property. Where he lived is not stated, but as R. Joshua quotes in *Sotah*, V, 1, to R. Akiba a statement of R. Zechariah, the latter seems to have lived in Jamnia. This is confirmed by his giving evidence with R. Josê the priest (*'Eduj.*, VIII, 2). As R. Eleazar b. R. Josê, who lived in the Darom, probably Lydda, reported some of his statements, one in *Tos. B. bath.*, VII, 10 (in b. 111 a, R. Josê b. R. Jehudah and R. Eleazar b. R. Josê, cf. *jer.*, VIII, 16 a, 17), and another in *Tos. Meg.*, I, 6, it is just as possible that he lived in Lydda.

[2] *ARN*, VI, 15 b; 2 *ARN*, XIII, 15 b; *Genes. r.*, 42, 1; *Pirkê R. Eliezer*, I.

[3] *Synh.*, 68 a; *Berakh.*, 16 b; *jer.*, II, 5 b, 66; *Semaḥ.*, I, 10.

he had also a female slave (*Berakh.*, 16 b; *Semaḥ.*, I, 10), a vineyard (*Tos. Ma'as. sh.*, V, 16; *Rosh haShan.*, 31 b), fields planted with flax, olive-trees, and date-palms (*Synh.*, 101 a).[1] R. Eliezer's wife, Imma Shalom, sent as bribe a golden candlestick to a philosopher who boasted incorruptibility, and brought a fictitious civil case concerning her inheritance before him (*Sabb.*, 116 a, b). Her brother, R. Gamaliel II, the president of the beth-din in Jamnia after R. Joḥanan b. Zakkai, was a wealthy man. The style of living in his house was that of a rich man, his rooms were furnished with sofas for dinner (*Tos. Jom tob*, II, 13), guests dined with him on holy days, among whom were R. Ṣadok and his son Eleazar (*Beṣah*, 22 b, 23 a, and parallels); after dinner smelling spices were burnt, for holy days the scent was prepared beforehand and kept in boxes (*Tos. Jom tob*, II, 14; *jer. Beṣah*, II, 61 c, 57, 59, *b.* 22 b); special kinds of food were prepared in his house, some with Greek names (*Tos.*, II, 16, *jer.*, II, 61 d, 18. *b.* 22 b). As he gave tithes (*Ma'as. sheni*, V, 9), he had landed property[2]; he had for his fields

[1] In a Baraitha in *Sabb.*, 127 b, a man of Upper Galilee served for three years with a farmer in the Darom. At the conclusion of his service on the eve of the Day of Atonement, he asked for his wages in order to return home and to provide for his wife and his children. The master replied that he had neither money, nor produce, nor field, nor cattle, saddles, or cushions, which the servant asked in succession. He took his luggage and, greatly disappointed, went home. After the feast of Tabernacles the master took the servant's wages, a load of three asses of food, drink, and sweet things, and took all this to his former servant. In the conversation it turned out that the servant had thought his master had expended all his money on cheap articles for business, his cattle had been hired by somebody, his field leased, his produce had not been tithed yet, and all his other possessions consecrated to God. The master then explained that, in order to force his son Hyrkanos to study Torah, he had prohibited himself by a vow the use of all his property, but now his vow was annulled by his colleagues in the Darom. This scholar, living in the Darom, father of a Hyrkanos, and having relations with Upper Galilee, is evidently R. Eliezer b. Hyrkanos, as She'iltoth, *Exodus*, § 40, in the same report expressly state, and give as the name of the servant Akiba b. Josef. Though the source of this is unknown to me, the Baraitha itself, with its references to property of all kinds in Lydda, deserves special attention.

[2] A female slave of his was once baking loaves of priestly due, and

several farmers (אריסים, *B. meṣ.*, V, 8) to whom he advanced wheat to be returned in kind and to be reckoned at the lowest price. He engaged labourers for working his fields whom he fed with produce bought from a Jew and not certainly tithed.[1] R. Akiba was a wealthy man, as he himself said to the crowd attending his son's funeral (*Semaḥ.*, VIII), and there are various legends accounting for his great wealth.[2] To satisfy both opinions in the controversy of the schools, he gave two tithes of citrons which he collected, evidently in his own garden (*Tos. Shebi.*, IV, 21; *Rosh haShan.*, 14 a). A colleague of R. Akiba in the school, R. Jesheb'ab distributed all his property among the poor, and R. Gamaliel sent him the message that the rabbis approved only of a fifth of one's possessions to be given away.[3] Where he lived and the kind of his property is not defined; but in *Nazir*, 65 a, a Baraitha says: Once R. Jesheb'ab examined a field for human bodies and found two which had been noticed before, and one that had not been noticed, and on this he proposed to declare the field a place of tombs, but R. Akiba told him: All your work is useless, for only three known or three discovered bodies constitute sufficient evidence. He lived, as other evidence shows, in Jamnia or Lydda, and probably owned land; as he can only have

another time she was stopping jugs of wine of such due (*Niddah*, 6 b). *RŠBM* and *Tosafoth* refer this to R. Gamaliel I, though as a rule he is called Gamaliel the Old; in *jer. Niddah*, II, 49 d, 36, the wine was for libations in the Temple.

[1] *Dammai*, III, 1. The Jew was not trustworthy in matters of tithes and priestly dues. Such landowners were termed 'Am ha'areṣ, as we find R. Ṣadok asking R. Joshua whether a distinction was made between Ḥaber and 'Am ha'areṣ as to blemishes of a firstborn animal (*Bekhor.*, 36 a); and also in a discussion between Shammaiites and Hillelites, here R. Eliezer and R. Joshua, about levitical purity (*Ḥag.*, 22 a, b; *'Eduj.*, I, 14).

[2] *Nedar.*, 50 a, b; *ARN*, VI, 15 a, b; 2 *ARN*, XII, 15 b, describe his furniture of gold and a jewel of his wife.

[3] *Jer. Pe'ah*, I, 15 b, 39; a Baraitha in *Kethub.*, 50 a, merely reports: A man wanted to give away more than a fifth of his property, but his colleague would not allow it; some say that it was R. Jesheb'ab and R. Akiba.

examined Jewish property, we learn of such in Judaea.[1] A friend of R. Eleazar b. 'Azarjah was Boethos b. Zonen in Lydda; in his house we find R. Gamaliel and his colleagues in the night of a Passover discussing laws of the feast (*Tos. Pesaḥ.*, X, 12), and as R. Jehudah reports (*Tos. Pesaḥ.*, I, 31; *jer.*, II, 29 c, 1; *b.* 37 a), he asked in Jamnia of R. Gamaliel and the rabbis a question about unleavened cakes for the same feast. At the advice of R. Eleazar b. 'Azarjah, he had eight books of the prophets bound together (*B. bathra*, 13 b, bottom). Once he brought in a ship dried figs on which heathen wine from a broken barrel came (*'Ab. zar.*, V, 2); the rabbis permitted the figs. He lent money to Jews and took their fields for pledges on the condition that, in case the debt would not be paid on the appointed day, the field should be sold to him; to avoid even an appearance of interest, he consulted R. Eleazar b. 'Azarjah as to the procedure (*B. meṣ.*, V, 3; *b.* 63 a; *Tos.*, IV, 2; *jer.*, V, 10 b, 13).[2] This precaution shows that his debtors were Jews, and we learn another instance of property in Jewish hands.[3]

A few decisions of rabbis as judges in civil and other suits also prove that Jews in Judaea owned not merely landed property, but also other means. A man who had promised his wife in her marriage settlement 400 zuzs in case of divorce, vowed that he would not live with her. At the complaint of his wife, R. Akiba upheld her claim to the full amount. When the man explained that his

[1] To this may be added the legend in Hegesippus (Eusebius, *Hist. Eccl.*, III, 20) in which the relatives of Jesus were questioned by Domitian as to their financial position, and they answered: 'We both possess only 900 denars, of which a half belongs to each, and even this we possess not in cash, but in land consisting of 39 plethras.'

[2] Another instance of lending money on fields is found in R. Akiba's advice to his disciple R. Simeon b. Joḥai in *Pesaḥ.*, 112 b, top: If you want to do a good deed and at the same time profit by it, lend money to your fellow on a field to enjoy its income as instalment, and the borrower has also a profit from your money.

[3] R. Jehudah in *Tos. Sabb.*, III, 4, reports that Boethos had a bucket of water prepared on Friday to have it poured over him on the Sabbath.

father had left to him and his brother altogether only 800 denars, so that he was unable to pay the amount, R. Akiba replied: Even if you should have to sell your hair, you must pay the marriage settlement (*Nedar.*, IX, 5). A man who offended a woman by uncovering her head in the street was fined 400 zuzs by R. Akiba; when he, later on, proved that the woman herself, when seeing a jug of smelling oil poured out in front of her house, had uncovered her head in the street, R. Akiba adhered to his decision (*B. kam.*, VIII, 6). In the first case the money seems to have passed after the year 70 from the father to the son, and must have been saved in spite of the Roman conquest. In the second case, the amount of the fine shows the standard of wealth and of private honour. R. Gamaliel fined a man ten gold pieces for covering in anticipation the blood of a fowl slaughtered by another man, and thus depriving him of the merit of a religious act (*Ḥull.*, 87 a).[1] There were in Judaea wealthy people, as we read that R. Akiba, who lived in Lydda and later in benê-Berak, showed honour to such (*'Erub.*, 86 a). They owned land, produce, cattle, and money; and it is noteworthy that the property could be sold or passed on as a gift or inheritance, showing the right of free disposition and fullest ownership. Josephus's statement that Vespasian declared the land of the province his private property that was to be leased (*Wars*, VII, 6, 6; Schürer, *Geschichte*, I, 640), will have to be referred to the towns and villages conquered by force, but not to those that had surrendered and were not deprived of their property; or the Romans sold the conquered land to any Jew for a nominal price, holding the new owner responsible for the taxes, as it mattered to them nothing who possessed the land, if only the taxes were paid. For this purpose it was

[1] A man bought something from one of two men, but did not know from which, and both claimed the price; R. Tarfon advised him to put the purchase-money between both and go away. R. Akiba said there was no other solution but to pay both, *B. kam.*, 103 b.

the law that no property could change hands without registration at the competent Roman office, as several passages in the Talmud and Midrash clearly state.[1]

4. There were, naturally, also poor people in Judaea, in the first instance many orphans whose parents had either fallen in the War or were taken captive and sold. For in the upper chamber of R. Tarfon it was resolved, after a discussion between the assembled rabbis, that Psalm cvi. 3 b, Blessed is he who practises charity at all times, enjoined the duty to bring up an orphan in one's house.[2] There were other poor who had inherited no property from their fathers, as R. Joshua b. Ḥananjah, who earned a living by making charcoal (*Berakh.*, 28 a), or needles (*jer.*, IV, 7 d, 20)[3] and who once reproached the head of the school, R. Gamaliel, that he knew nothing of the troubles of scholars in earning a living[4]; his house

[1] Baraitha *'Ab. zar.*, 13 a; *Tos.*, I, 8, speaks of slaves, male and female, of houses, fields, and vineyards, purchased and brought before the office of non-Jews; similarly *Tos. 'Ab. zar.*, VI, 2; Baraitha *Gitt.*, 44 a; *Tos. B. bathra*, VIII, 2; *Sifrê Num.*, 117. As the office is already mentioned by R. Akiba in Baraitha *Gitt.*, 11 a; *Tos.*, I, 4 (see my *'Am ha'areṣ*, 244, 37), those passages could not very well be referred to Galilee after the year 135.

[2] *Midrash Esther*, VI begin. on 2, 5, and *Midr. Psalms*, 106, 3, see Buber, and Bacher, *Tannaiten*, I, 188, 4. As R. Eleazar of Modeim is asked to give his opinion, the discussion took place in R. Tarfon's time; in *Kethub.*, 50 a, the interpretation is quoted in the name of R. Samuel b. Naḥman. In *Midr. Proverbs*, 6, 20, R. Meir asks Elisha b. 'Abuja, his teacher, whether there is a remedy for an adulteress, and Elisha cites a statement of ben-'Azzai, his colleague, who recommended as a remedy for such a woman the bringing up of an orphan in her house and teaching him Torah and observance.

[3] In spite of his poverty he received a wayfarer whom he provided with food and drink, and, as he had no room for him, he took him to the roof of his house (*Derekh 'ereṣ*, V, end). About midnight the stranger stole all things which he found on the roof, and not knowing that his host had removed the steps, tried to descend and broke his collar-bone.

[4] A worse case was that of Naḥum of Gimzô (*Ta'an.*, 21 a) who, deprived of the use of his limbs, arms, eyes, and visited by leprosy, lived in a house in very bad repairs. For his terrible condition he accounted to his disciples as follows: When once on my way to my father-in-law with three asses laden with food, drink, and sweet things, I met a poor man who asked for my help; while I unloaded my ass, the man died and I cursed my limbs and my body.

was small, but had a gate in which once four scholars sat and studied (*Tos. Berakh.*, IV, 18). Especially in the first years after the War the struggle must have been very hard, as is evident from a statement of R. Ḥaninah, the vice high priest (*ARN*, XX, 36 a): he who takes the Torah to heart, is relieved of many fears, the first of them being the fear of hunger. This is explained in full to mean: when one craves for a piece of barley-bread or a drop of vinegar or drink, or would like to put on a shirt of wool or linen, he does not possess it, everything is lacking; we are without a lamp, a knife, and a table.[1] R. Ishmael on one occasion said (*Nedar.*, IX, 10): Jewish girls are handsome, but poverty disfigures them. The Roman governor asked R. Akiba why God did not maintain the poor in Israel if He loved them (*B. bathra*, 10 a); he evidently based his question on actual conditions in Judaea.[2] It is related in a Baraitha[3] that the burial of a dead relative was, owing to the expenses, a greater trouble to the family than his death, so that some left the dead and fled, till R. Gamaliel expressed the wish to be buried in plain linen, when everybody followed his example. Though some scholars refer this to R. Gamaliel I, between the years 30 and 50, the name without the distinctive adjective 'the old' and the poverty are in favour of R. Gamaliel II. Poor students belonged to the school of Jamnia (*Sifrê Deut.*, 16; *Horaj.*, 10 a, b) who were supported by wealthy scholars

[1] Of R. Gamaliel's household it is said in *Sabb.*, 113 a, bottom, *Tos.*, XII, 16, that they did not fold their garments on the Sabbath, because they had another set to change; it seems to imply that ordinary people had only one set.

[2] R. Akiba terms poverty an ornament of Israel (*Lev. r.*, 35, 6), but says that even the poor are nobles (*B. kam.*, VIII, 6); he himself walked, when he was a scholar, bare-footed even in Rome, and was jeered at by an eunuch (*Koh. r.*, 10, 7), and enjoined on his son Joshua among other things not to withhold shoes from his feet (*Pesaḥ.*, 112 a; Bacher, *Tannaiten*, I, 270, 2). It is not evident whether he did so owing to poverty. R. Tarfon wore shoes, *Tos. Neg.*, VIII, 2; *Sifra*, 70 c; *jer. Sotah*, II, 18 a, 7.

[3] *Kethub.*, 8 b; *Tos. Nid.*, IX, 17; *jer. Berakh.*, III, 6 a, 34; *Semaḥ.*, XIV, end.

such as R. Tarfon (p. 33) and Neḥunjah b. Hakanah (*Megil.*, 28 a), and sometimes invited to dinner by their masters (*Derekh 'ereṣ*, VII). Some support was obtained by collections, great scholars not minding to journey for such purpose to distant towns (*jer. Horaj.*, III, 48 a, 44), and wealthy Jews contributing liberally. Characteristic is the statement of Naḥum of Gimzô that his old age was due to his never having accepted presents (*Meg.*, 28 a).

5. It may be safely assumed that the landowning Jews in Judaea worked their fields as strenuously as before the War, as their taxes had increased owing to the revolution and living was under direct Roman rule not easier. Incidentally we hear of very early work in the field.[1] Whether the Wars left the Jew in possession of sufficient working animals, cows, and asses, is not evident from the scanty records. R. Eleazar b. 'Azarjah had very numerous herds, and he probably was no exception. Besides, there are in connexion with priestly dues a few references to cows and sheep. The rabbis permitted 'Ela in Jamnia to charge four asses for his examination of a firstborn sheep or goat, and six for a calf, no difference whether it was found to be with or without blemish (*Bekhor.*, IV, 5). R. Ṣadok the priest had a firstborn animal (*Bekhor.*, 36 a; *Berakh.*, 27 b); R. Gamaliel had one, the lower jaw of which was larger than the upper, and this anomaly was declared a blemish (*Bekhor.*, VI, 9). About the nature of another blemish in the house of Menaḥem R. Akiba and R. Joḥanan b. Nuri differed

[1] R. Eliezer in *Cant. r.*, introduction, § 9, said: Nobody ever was before me in the house of learning or left by me there; once I rose early and already met the manure- and straw-labourers, they were early workers; should not we be at our work as early as they? Bacher, *Tannaiten*, I, 101, 3. The rabbis worked all day long in their respective occupations, and in the evening they attended the school, even on Friday and holy day night, *Tos. Sabb.*, V, 13; *Sifrê Num.*, 116; *Pesaḥ.*, 72 b. R. Tarfon, *Pesaḥ.*, 109 a R. Akiba, *Tos. Beṣah*, II, 16 R. Jehudah b. Baba and R. Simeon of Timnah. On some occasions also ordinary people were present in greater numbers, *Berakh.*, 27 b; *jer.*, IV, 7 d, 5, 6, if העם means such, and not the usual audience of scholars.

(VI, 6; b. 40a; *Tos.*, IV, 8). A Baraitha in *Synh.*, 33 a, reports another case in the same house: R. Tarfon declared a cow without matrix unsuitable for food and gave it to the dogs; when the matter was brought before the teachers in Jamnia, Theodos, the doctor, said that no cow or sow left Alexandria without its matrix being first removed to prevent it from bearing (IV, 4). A cow expired on a holy day, and R. Tarfon brought the question before the school whether the removal of the carcass was permitted, and of priestly due that was defiled (*Beṣah*, III, 5). R. Gamaliel had cattle, for his son Simeon said (*Tos. Sabb.*, XV, 2; b. 128b): We used to stimulate the maternal instinct of a clean animal on a holy day. R. Simeon of Timnah slaughtered on a holy day a calf, to appease a troop of soldiers (*Tos. Beṣah*, II, 6; b. 21a). Abba Saul relates (*Tos. Sabb.*, IX, 21; *Jebam.*, 114a): We used to suck milk from a clean animal on a holy day. It is noteworthy that the wealthy R. Gamaliel had only just as many cows as the working of his fields required; for when the wedding feast of his son was to be prepared, he had to buy some cattle in the market of Emmaus (*Ḥull.*, 91 b, and parallels).[1]

It must not be forgotten that R. Eliezer was asked by his disciples whether sheep and goats may be reared, and that he gave an evasive answer (*Tos. Jebam.*, III, 4), while R. Gamaliel replied to the same question of his disciples in the affirmative.[2] Perhaps the Shammaiite R. Eliezer would not abolish even a temporary pro-

[1] We find rabbis riding on asses, as R. Joḥanan b. Zakkai in *Kethub.*, 66 b; *Sifrê Deut.*, 305; *Ḥag.*, 14 b, and parallels; R. Gamaliel riding from Akko to Ekdippa in *'Erub.*, 64 b; *Tos. Pesaḥ.*, 1, 28; *jer. 'Abod. zar.*, I, 40 a, 65. An ass of R. Gamaliel was loaded for too many hours with honey and died, *Sabb.*, 154 b. R. Gamaliel gave a Libyan ass as bribe to a philosopher and judge who pretended to be incorruptible, *Sabb.*, 116 b. When finding that he will have to pay for the consequences of a wrong judgment, R. Tarfon said: Thy ass is gone, Tarfon, *Synh.*, 33 a. Doves in Lydda are mentioned in *Tos. Tohar.*, IX, 14; a dove-cote in Lydda in *Tos. Berakh.*, IV, 16; *Mekhiltha*, 31 b.

[2] *B. kam.*, 80 a, top, and my *'Am ha'areṣ*, 191 ff.

hibition in spite of changed conditions, while R. Gamaliel the Hillelite had no hesitation to do so. It cannot be accidental that no flocks were mentioned of any rabbi or landowner discussed above; and it is most instructive that in the exhaustive enumeration of goods and possessions in the house of a wealthy farmer in Judaea in the Baraitha in *Sabb.*, 127 b, herds, but not flocks, are included, fully in accordance with R. Eliezer who is meant there (p. 37, note 1). Professor Krauss [1] tried by every possible argument to dispute the fact implied by the questions addressed to R. Eliezer and R. Gamaliel and to show that the prohibition to rear sheep and goats was mere theory; but arguments cannot remove clear reports of facts. Though we may be able to point to instances of sheep reared,[2] we have to consider that R. Gamaliel had permitted it and 'Ela, the examiner of blemishes of firstborn sheep or goats, acted as such in Jamnia. There may have been farmers in Judaea who, even before R. Gamaliel's permission, reared flocks; but that is no proof against the prohibition and its general observance, as we find only herdsmen referred to incidentally with R. Tarfon (*'Erub.*, 45 a), but no shepherds.[3] The fact that the prohibition of rearing flocks is put together with that of cutting down fruit-bearing trees, suggests some inner connexion between the two, in so far as the protection of newly-planted trees, necessitated by the devastation of the country by the Romans, implied the prohibition of rearing especially goats.[4]

[1] *Revue des Études Juives*, 1907, LIII, 14 ff.

[2] In a Baraitha in *Sabb.*, 53 b, R. Jehudah reports that the family of Antiochia had goats with large breasts and had to tie bags on them to prevent their wounding them. Perhaps that family lived in Lydda or Jamnia.

[3] In *Kiddush.*, 82 a, Abba Gorja says that no one should train his son to be an ass- or camel-driver, nor a coachman or a boatman, herdsman or grocer, because their occupation implies dishonesty. He seems to make no distinction between herds and flocks; but from the several references to shepherds as robbers it is probable that he referred in the first instance to shepherds.

[4] See also the report in the tractate of *Kallah*, ed. Coronel, 19 a: Once

6. The success of the most careful farming depended to a very great extent on rain in proper time. R. Simeon b. Gamaliel, in the name of R. Joshua, said (*Sotah*, IX, 12): Since the day of the destruction of the Temple there has been no day without a curse, and dew has not come down for blessing, and the taste of the produce has been taken away. R. Joshua had known the years immediately preceding the destruction of Jerusalem, and though the bitterness of the fruit may largely have been due to the bitter mood of the Jews, he must have noticed some change in the produce.[1] R. Eleazar b. Parta, who lived before the year 135, said in a Baraitha (*Ta'an.*, 19 b): Since the day of the destruction of the Temple, rains have become scanty in the world; there are years when rains are abundant, others when they are too little, in some they come in time, in others out of season. Samuel the Young, a member of the school in Jamnia, instituted public fasts on two occasions, obviously for rain to come (*Ta'an.*, 25 b); in Lydda the authorities, owing to a drought, ordered a fast on the feast of Ḥanukkah, but R. Eliezer and R. Joshua refused to recognize it.[2] R. Eliezer and R. Akiba instituted public fasts and rain came down (*Ta'an.*, 25 b; *jer.*, III, 66 c, 76); when once a fast was held in Lydda and rain came down before noon, R. Tarfon allowed the people to go and to eat and to drink and to have a holiday (*Ta'an.*, III, 9). In a year of drought, R. Tarfon betrothed to himself several women to enable them to eat of his priestly due

R. Akiba sat at his table under an olive-tree owing to religious persecutions, and said: Those who rear small cattle and cut down good trees, and children's teachers who do not do their work properly, will see no sign of blessing (see also *Pesaḥ.*, 50 b). The persuasive tone of the statement suggests that some people were acting against the prohibition.

[1] Judaean wine never turned sour in the times of the Temple, but it did so in R. Jehudah's days, *jer. Dammai*, I, 21 d, 8; *Tos.*, I, 2; b. *Pesaḥ.*, 42 b. R. Eliezer never suffered any loss by his wine turning sour, or by his flax being smitten, or his oil smelling badly, or his honey fermenting, *Synh.*, 101 a.

[2] *Tos. Ta'an.*, II, 5; *jer.*, II, 66 a, 44; *b. Rosh haShan.*, 18 b.

(*Tos. Kethub.*, V, 1; *jer. Jebam.*, IV, 6 b, 59); and in such a year Joshua, the son of R. Akiba, made special arrangements with his rich wife (*Tos. Kethub.*, IV, 7; *jer.*, V, 29 d, 25).[1] Drought often entailed for many starvation and death; when once R. Eliezer prayed at a public fast meeting for rain, and in spite of several fasts his prayer was not fulfilled, he said to the congregation: Have you prepared graves for yourselves (*Ta'an.*, 25 b)? The land was fertile, especially so in the western districts of Judaea. R. Jehudah, by birth a Galilean, who attended the schools in Lydda, Jamnia, and benê-Berak, says (*B. bath.*, 122 a): A se'ah of land in Judaea is worth five se'ahs in Galilee. And his colleague, R. Josê of Sepphoris, says in a Baraitha (*Kethub.*, 112 a): A se'ah of field in Judaea yielded five se'ahs, one of fine flour, one of sifted fine flour, one of bran, one of coarse bran, and one of cibarium.[2] R. Jacob b. Dosithai tells (*Kethub.*, 111 b, bottom) how he once, early in the morning, walked from Lydda to 'Onô to his ankles in honey of figs.[3] The produce of the fields in ordinary years seems to have been sufficient for maintaining the population in spite of the heavy taxes in

[1] R. Jehudah speaks of a year of drought when men in places left their Lulabs to their sons as inheritance (*Tos. Suk.*, II, 9); perhaps it was the same year when on his sea voyage with R. Joshua, R. Eleazar b. 'Azarjah, and R. Akiba, only R. Gamaliel had a Lulab which he had bought for a thousand zuzs (*Suk.*, 41 b). There seem to have been unsatisfactory years not due to drought; for R. Joshua accounts by special sins for the lack of blessing in produce and for man's toil not being rewarded by sufficient food (*ARN*, XXXVIII, 57 a). R. Eliezer's or R. Ishmael's remark that when the Jews do not fulfil God's will they are compelled to keep four years of rest instead of the one prescribed (*Mekhil.*, 23, p. 100 b), also suggests sad times.

[2] The parallel in *jer. Pe'ah*, VII, 20 a, 70, by R. Ḥijja b. 'Abba, does not mention Judaea. The price of land is nowhere stated, except in the legend of Hegesippus about Jesus' relatives (p. 39, n. 1), where they state their property to be 900 denarii in the shape of 39 plethra of land. Though the historical value of the report is very doubtful, it may have been made up on real conditions in Palestine of the time of Hegesippus, when 1 plethra of land was worth $23\frac{3}{39}$ denarii.

[3] Rabbi once came to benê-Berak and saw lying there a cluster as big as a calf of three years; *Midrash Tannaim*, ed. Hoffmann, 173 ff.

kind to be considered below.[1] As there were many without land, they had to buy provisions in the market; and we learn that R. Eleazar b. 'Azarjah dealt in wine and oil for many years (*B. bath.*, 91, a; *Tos. 'Ab. zar.*, IV, 1). Of export, we hear only in a discussion between R. Jehudah b. Bethera and another teacher. Boethos b. Zonen brought from outside, by ship, dried figs (*'Ab. zar.*, V, 2), perhaps in a year of drought.

7. A passing reference to the food of the Jews in the period considered may be of some interest. R. Eleazar b. 'Azarjah, in a sentence preserved in two forms, prescribes food according to one's means (*Tos. 'Arakh.*, IV, 27): He who owns 10 manahs, may eat every day vegetables boiled in a pot; if he has 20 manahs, he may eat the same vegetables first boiled and then stewed; if he has 50 manahs, he may buy every Friday a pound of meat; if he has 100 manahs, he may have a pound of meat every day. In the parallel (*Ḥull.*, 84 a) it reads differently: He who has 1 manah, may buy for his pot one pound of vegetables, with 10 manahs a pound of fish for his pot, with 50 manahs a pound of meat, if he has 100 manahs, let a pot (of meat) be put up on the fire for him every day. The difference is not due merely to varying traditions, but, it seems, to different parts of Palestine, which cannot be investigated here. The pupils of R. Tarfon ate of his beets, raw ones, with or without salt (*Nedar.*, 49 b), but sometimes also meat with eggs; for R. Jehudah reports (*Nedar.*, VI, 6) that when they—in the *Baraitha Nedar.*, 52 b, he—once vowed not to eat meat, R. Tarfon prohibited them—or him—to eat even eggs boiled with meat. What caused this vow would be interesting, but is not suggested. As was shown above (p. 44), R. Gamaliel had to go to the market in Emmaus to buy cattle for the wedding feast of his son (*Ḥull.*, 91 b), as eating meat was an essential expression of joy; and R. Josê reports (*Bekhor.*, 40 a; *Tos.*,

[1] R. Gamaliel bought corn from a Jew who seemed unreliable as to giving tithes, and fed his labourers with it, *Dammai*, III, 1.

IV, 8) that in the house of a certain Menaḥem a cow was slaughtered, but no special occasion is mentioned. In R. Gamaliel's house, various dishes with Greek names are incidentally referred to (*Tos. Beṣah*, II, 16; *jer.*, II, 61 d, 18), to which pepper was used; but even on a festival a bucketful of lentils was in his house one of the dishes (*Beṣah*, 14 b; *Tos.*, I, 22), and fish is also mentioned once as brought to R. Gamaliel (*Beṣah*, III, 2). Akylas the proselyte had a man-cook who once brought a levitical question before the school of R. Gamaliel (*Tos. Kelim*, 3, II, 4), as Akylas kept his food in high levitical purity (*Tos. Ḥag.*, III, 3). R. Joshua, when on a journey in lodgings, lived on beans (*ʽErub.*, 53 b), other teachers on vegetables. Wine, as far as incidental remarks allow judgment, was almost as rare as meat. At the wedding feast of his son, R. Akiba offered freely wine to his guests (*Tos. Sabb.*, VII, 9; b. 67 b; *jer. Berakh.*, VI, 10 d, 58), as it was done at every festivity (משתה, *Kiddush.*, 32 b, *Sifrê Deut.*, 38). In the houses of wealthy people wine may have been more usual (*Berakh.*, VIII, 1 ff., and *jer.*, VI, 10, c, 76 ff. concerning סעודה), so that R. Gamaliel and his companion drank wine on the way from Akko to Ekdippa (*ʽErub.*, 64 b, and parallels). Bread was made of wheat; barley as every-day food of a wife was, according to R. José, permitted only by R. Ishmael, who lived near Idumaea (*Kethub.*, V, 8); on the festivals, as on Passover, more luxurious cakes were baked, as R. Akiba made on the Passover for R. Eliezer and R. Joshua a dough with oil and honey (*Pesaḥ.*, 36 a). As Joshua, R. Akiba's disciple, was a grit-miller (*ʽErub.*, 21 b), grits must have been common food.

All the food mentioned was in most cases derived from one's own field and required no outlay of money. Those who were compelled to buy provisions, had first to earn some money. R. Gamaliel engaged Jews as labourers (p. 38), and in addition to their food must have paid them some wages. Of trade, hardly any clear evidence is found, though there must have been grocers and bakers. R. Eleazar b. 'Azarjah dealt in wine and oil (*B. bathra*, 91, a; *Tos. 'Ab. zar.*, IV, 1); R. Jehudah was a baker, and bakers' shops are mentioned in *Tos. 'Ahil.*, XVIII, 18; *Jadaj.*, II, 16, and Joshua a grit-miller (*'Erub.*, 21 b). Lydda had vendors who sold their goods dear (*B. meṣ.*, IV, 3), and a synagogue of weavers or metal-workers (*Nazir*, 52 a, and parallels). R. Joshi'a gave up his studies and took up business, for which his colleague R. Matthia blamed him (*ARN*, I, 1 a), and R. Akiba seems to have been connected with shipping (*Nedar.*, 50a, b). A R. Joḥanan was sandal-maker (*Sifrê Deut.*, 80; *Midrasch Tannaim*, 58); a Jehudah a perfumer (*Ḥull.*, 55 b, and parallel); Simeon a cotton-dealer (?); R. Ishmael a Torah-writer (*Sotah*, 20 a); and Eleazar a writer (*Ḥull.*, 55 b); and in connexion with the deposition of R. Gamaliel, a fuller is mentioned (*jer. Berakh.*, IV, 7 d, 23).[1]

8. As almost natural after the terrible catastrophe, the mood of the Jews of Judaea was depressed. Not only immediately after the destruction of the Temple and of the country, when some men, on account of the sanctuary, resolved not to eat meat and not to drink wine, and R. Joshua had to dissuade them (*B. bath.*, 60 b; *Tos. Sotah*, XV, 11)[2]; and when the author of the *Apocalypse of Baruch* voiced the despair of some religious

[1] The rabbis urged the Jews to teach their children a craft; R. Gamaliel describes it as giving security, *Tos. Kiddush.*, I, 11, and R. Ishmael in *jer. Pe'ah*, I, 15 c, top, explains 'choose life' in Deut. xxx. 19 to refer to a craft. Judaea had places engaged in the wool industry, not only women working in their household (*B. kam.*, X, 9), but, as R. Hosha'jah in the first half of the third century reports (*Tanḥuma*, נשוא, 8, see Buber, § 14, note 70), there were villages in the Darom engaged in dyeing purple, and there most men had dyed hands. See for the fourth century 'Totius urbis descriptio' (Müller, *Geographi Graeci minores*, II, 513; Schürer, *Geschichte*, II, 56, 173), which mentions Lydda, Neapolis, Caesarea, Sarepta 'purpuram praestant'.

[2] Also R. Ishmael said in *B. bath.*, 60 b, bottom; *Tos. Sotah*, XV, 10, that we ought to abstain from everything, but it could not be carried out by the people. R. Joshua himself had at first to be comforted by his teacher R. Joḥanan b. Zakkai in *ARN*, IV, 11 a; 2 *ARN*, VIII, 11 b.

leaders and of a section of the population. But also later, when a recognized authority gave expression to the feelings of the people by prescribing for joyful occasions some signs of mourning, the same mood still prevailed. For *Mishnah Sotah*, IX, 14, reports: In the war of Vespasian a decree was issued concerning wreaths of bridegrooms and the drum (*b.* 49 b; *jer.*, IX, 24 c, 4)[1]; and *Tos. Sotah*, XV, 7, says: Since the Synedrion ceased, song ceased in the house of feasting. It is true, we find that the book of Canticles was sung as an ordinary song at feasts, and R. Akiba denounced such songs in the strongest terms[2]; but the section of the population that feasted in this way did not seem to share the general feeling in this as in other respects. Other constant and spontaneous reminders of the loss of Jerusalem were suggested by a rabbi, probably R. Joshua: One may whitewash his house and leave merely a spot not whitewashed in memory of Jerusalem; one may prepare everything for a dinner and leave one thing out in memory of Jerusalem; a woman may adorn herself and leave one ornament in memory of Jerusalem.[3] The strict observance of the 9th of 'Ab, the day of the destruction

[1] Of feasting at circumcisions and weddings we read in the Baraitha *Synh.*, 32 b; *jer. Kethub.*, I, 25 c, 32; *Tos. Sabb.*, VII, 9, and elsewhere, p. 49.

[2] *Tos. Synh.*, XII, 10; in an anonymous Baraitha in *Synh.*, 101 a, R. Joshua b. Ḥananjah denounces the same; in *ARN*, XXXVI, 54 b, it is ascribed to R. Joḥanan b. Nuri.

[3] *Tos. Sotah*, end; *B. bath.*, 60 b; Bacher, *Tannaiten*, I, 159, 3. Other things of luxury ceased to be used, as white glass. Though in the report in Baraitha *Sotah*, 48 b: Since the destruction of the first Temple the use of Pranda silk, of white glass and iron chariots ceased, according to some also the jelly of wine from Senir that resembled fig-cakes, this is connected with the destruction of the first Temple (cf. *jer. Sukkah*, IV, 54 d, 13), it is evident from Baraitha *Moëd kat.*, 27 a, bottom; *jer. Dammai*, IV, 24 a, 66; *Tos. Niddah*, IX, 17, that the second Temple was meant. For first wealthy people went to comfort mourners with wine in bottles of white glass, the poor in such of coloured glass, and as the poor were hereby put to shame, it was instituted that everybody should use coloured glass. This institution and the others reported there belong to a very late period of the second Temple.

of Jerusalem,[1] the mourning for the Temple (*Threni r.*, I, 2; IV *Ezra* 9, 38 ff.), the inclusion of a special prayer for the restoration of the holy city in the eighteen benedictions,[2] all show the mood of the people and the endeavour of the rabbis to strengthen the hope of the Jews for the restoration of Jerusalem and the Temple.

9. In conclusion a few words must be said about the life and the position of women in Judaea between the years 70 and 135. The very strange discussion as to whether one is legally bound to maintain his small children, suggests terrible poverty. R. Eliezer declared it a good deed to feed one's little sons and daughters (*Kethub.*, 50 a), while R. Eleazar b. 'Azarjah formulated the law in the gathering of the rabbis in Jamnia that little daughters had no claim to maintenance (*Kethub.*, IV, 6). When a man refused to marry his niece, who was ugly, R. Ishmael said that all Jewish girls were bright, but poverty made them ugly (*Nedar.*, IX, 10). All men married, Simeon b. 'Azzai was an exception condemned by himself and R. Eliezer.[3] As a rule girls married after attaining puberty (*Pesaḥ.*, 112 a, b) and later; but we find also a child married to a man, so in the case of R. Ishmael's son (*jer. Jebam.*, XIII, 13 c, 19; *Nidd.*, 52 a), and another that came before R. Jehudah b. Baba (*Tos. Jebam.*, XIII, 5). R. Eliezer married his niece, who was an orphan and lived in his house, when she attained puberty (*ARN*, XVI, 32 a; in *jer. Jebam.*, XIII, 13 c, 60, before that time). To marry one's niece was commended and practised, and among others 'Abba had R. Gamaliel's, his brother's daughter, for a wife (*Jebam.*, 15 a), and he was the only instance reported to have had two wives.[4]

[1] *'Erub.*, 41 a; *Ta'an.*, 13 a; *jer. Beṣah*, II, 61 b, 51.

[2] Weiss, II, 73 ff.; Bacher, *Tannaiten*, I, 89.

[3] *Tos. Jebam.*, VIII, end; b. 63 b; *Genes. r.*, 34, 14; *Sotah*, 4 b.

[4] A very interesting question addressed to R. Eleazar b. R. Ṣadok by his disciples indicates an otherwise unknown, but very instructive fact: Why does everybody want to marry a proselyte, but not a freed maid-servant (*Horaj.*, 13 a)? We know only of few proselytes in Judaea in our period, and cannot account for the statement. Is it perhaps the Galilean R. Eleazar b. Ṣadok?

When R. Tarfon's wife died, he asked her sister in the cemetery to take charge of his children[1] and betrothed her. Once, when he saw a bridal procession pass by his school, he interrupted his teaching, brought the bride into his house and asked his mother and his wife to bathe, anoint, and adorn the bride, and then he danced before her and took her to her husband (*ARN*, XLI, 67 a). R. Ishmael persuaded a man to marry his niece who was poor and whom Ishmael's mother adorned for her wedding (*Nedar.*, IX, 10). Those girls had hardly any dowry, but there was the rich wife of R. Akiba's son who was maintained by his wife and studied (*Tos. Kethub.*, IV, 7, and parallel), and R. Eliezer's wife, the sister of R. Gamaliel. In a year of drought R. Tarfon betrothed to himself several women to enable them to eat of his priestly due (*Tos. Kethub.*, V, 1; *jer. Jebam.*, IV, 6 b, 59). The husband had to write to his wife a marriage settlement promising her at least 200 zuzs in case of divorce or his death, and that document protected her against whims of her husband (*Nedar.*, IX, 5) and made it for a poor man impossible to get rid of a tyrannical wife (*Genes. r.*, 17, 3). The son of R. Jehudah the baker, who had married his cousin, gave all property to her; but when his creditors claimed their money, she had to pay the debts and even her marriage settlement was lost (*B. bath.*, 132 a).[2] A married woman had to have her head covered in the street, and it was a serious offence to uncover it; R. Akiba fined a man heavily for it (*B. ḳam.*, VIII, 6). In moonlit evenings women met and in spinning discussed the latest events in the families of the place (*Gitt.*, 89 a); if they talk ugly things about a married woman, R. Akiba says, she must be divorced. And R. Joshua says (*Sotah*, VI, 1) that if a married woman was with

[1] *Jer. Jebam.*, IV, 6 b, 37; *Semaḥ.*, VII; *Moëd kat.*, 23 a.

[2] R. Akiba bought for his wife a golden ornament representing Jerusalem, *Sabb.*, 59 a, b; *jer.*, VI, 7 d, 65. When R. Gamaliel's wife envied her for it, her husband referred her to the great share which R. Akiba's wife had in his greatness.

another man alone and women spinning in the moonlight talk about it, she must be divorced (see *Sotah*, 6 b, bottom); R. Joḥanan b. Nuri objected most strongly to such evidence. Otherwise we find the wives and mothers of teachers in conversation with other rabbis, Imma Shalom, the wife of R. Eliezer (*Nedar.*, 20 b) and the mother of R. Ishmael and of R. Tarfon.[1] Women came to the schools with all kinds of religious questions,[2] and R. Ishmael and R. Eliezer asked their mother and wife respectively to examine girls as to their signs of puberty (*Tos. Nidd.*, VI, 8). R. Eliezer was once asked by a learned woman about a contradiction in the Bible, and his answer was: A woman's wisdom is in the distaff; in the parallel he replied: Words of the Torah should be burnt and not given to women.[3] He consistently prohibited to teach a girl Torah (*Sotah*, II, 4). R. Joshua's opinion was not favourable to women[4]: A woman is more satisfied with a kabh of food from her husband if intercourse is with it, than with nine kabhs of food and rare intercourse; a woman separating from intercourse is one of the destroyers of the world.[5] Whenever Pappos b. Jehudah left his house, he locked in his wife that she should not speak to anybody; but this is stated to have been an exception and wrong.[6] In the home the wife had to attend to the house and to its requirements, she had to look after her children (*jer. Jebam.*, IV, 6 b, 37), and, when free, she spun (*Kethub.*, V, 5); and we learn that she sold wool

[1] *Kiddush.*, 31 b; *jer.*, IV, 61 b, 18; *Nidd.*, 48 b; *Tos.*, VI, 8.

[2] *Tos. Kethub.*, IV, 7; *Niddah*, 48 b; VIII, 3; *Kethub.*, 10 b; *Jadaj.*, III, 1; *Ḥag.*, 20 a.

[3] *Joma*, 66 b; in *jer. Sotah*, III, 19 a, 5, the woman is a matrona, a non-Jewess.

[4] Little is known about the relations between rabbis and women of the people. R. Joshua once stayed with a woman who cooked his food (*'Erub.*, 53 b). When R. Ishmael died, the women of Israel bewailed him (*Nedar.*, IX, 10 ff.; *Baraitha*, 66 b).

[5] *Sotah*, III, 4; the translation of the word by separation from intercourse seems to me to follow from the context; see also *jer. Nedar.*, XI, 42 c, 65.

[6] Baraitha R. Meir in *Gitt.*, 90 a; *Tos. Sotah*, V, 9.

to dealers (*B. kam.*, X, 9; b. 119 a). Of children we hear little, only of the deaths of several young men, the son of R. Joḥanan b. Zakkai, when already a scholar (*ARN*, XIV, 29 b), of R. Ishmael's several sons (*Moëd k.*, 28 b), and of R. Akiba's son (*Semaḥ.*, VIII; *Moëd k.*, 21 b).[1] On the eve of Passover children were entertained with sweets by R. Tarfon or R. Akiba (*jer. Pesaḥ.*, X, 37 b, 75; b. 109 a). An anonymous Baraitha in *Jebam.*, 62 b, allows an insight into the principles practised by the teachers in their homes: To him who loves his wife as himself, and who honours her more than himself and guides his sons and his daughters in the straight way and who makes them marry immediately after puberty, applies Job v. 24.

III. The Political Conditions in Judaea and the Romans.

1. Though a great part of Judaea was saved in the catastrophe of the year 70, it did not escape an evil attending great wars; outlaws and robbers increased in number and enhanced the difficulties of maintenance and of recovery. Their place of activity was not only Galilee, where a son of R. Ḥaninah b. Teradjon of Sikhnin joined robbers and was ultimately killed by them as traitor (*Semaḥ.*, XII, *Threni r.*, 3, 16). But Judaea suffered even more from them, because there war followed war. When staying in Babylonia, in the lifetime of R. Gamaliel, on matters of intercalation, R. Akiba met in Neharde'a Nehemia of beth-Deli; they discussed the question of finding witnesses to testify to a man's death, and Nehemia referred R. Akiba to the fact that Judaea was infested with raiding bands (*Jebam.*, XVI, 7). In the neighbourhood of Lydda R. Tarfon was once in

[1] R. Akiba in *ARN*, XXVI, 41 b, in 2 *ARN*, XXXV, 41 a, Josê the Babylonian accounts for the death of young scholars; the frequency of the sad occurrence demanded an explanation. R. Akiba visited one of his disciples who was ill and visited by nobody (*Nedar.*, 40 a, 41 a).

danger of life when, according to Shammaiite rule, he lay down in the road to read a prayer (*Berakh.*, I, 3). A man told R. Tarfon how he and a companion were on the way pursued by a raiding band; his friend broke a branch from an olive-tree to use it as weapon and thereby invited the raiders to return, and was taken ill and died.[1] R. Jehudah relates[2] how a robber before his execution in Mazaga (Caesarea) in Cappadocia confessed to the murder of Simeon b. Kohen on entering Lydda; on this evidence Simeon's wife was allowed to re-marry. The informant's person shows that the case was discussed in Lydda or in Jamnia; as R. Akiba once stayed in Mazaga,[3] perhaps he brought the confession to Judaea before the schools. R. Joshua prescribed a short prayer to be said in a place of danger (*Berakh.*, IV, 4); though he prayed therein for help for the remnant of the nation בכל פרשת העבור, the parallel (*Berakh.*, 29 b; *Tos.*, III, 7) defines the danger as a troop of wild beasts and of robbers.[4] Some seem to have been Jews, as those who met R. Akiba's disciples on their way to Ekdippa (*'Ab. zar.*, 25 b). It is true, most of these instances of robbery and robbers in the Roman province of Judaea could belong to one special period of unrest, the war of Quietus in the year 116, when some revolutionary movement and persecutions on the part of the Romans again disturbed the country.[5]

[1] *Baraitha Jebam.*, 122 b; *Tos.*, XIV, 9, 10; *jer.*, XVI, 15 d, 38.

[2] *Baraitha Jebam.*, 25 b; *Tos.*, IV, 5; *jer.*, II, 4 b, 2.

[3] *Tos. Jebam.*, XIV, 5; *jer.*, XVI, 15 d, 14; b. 121 a. R. Akiba in *Semaḥ.*, IV, 34; *Derekh 'ereṣ z.*, VIII, relates how in his earlier days he once found a murdered man and carried the body 6,000 cubits till he reached a place of burial, and buried him. When he reported his act to the rabbis, they (R. Eliezer and R. Joshua) told him that he ought to have buried the man where he found him.

[4] Simeon of Timnah tells R. Jehudah b. Baba how the night before a troop of non-Jews came to his town and wanted to spoil the whole place; by slaughtering a young cow for them, they got rid of them in peace, *Beṣah*, 21 a; *Tos.*, II, 6. Rashi explains the Hebrew word as a great band of raiders who search everything; see the dictionaries.

[5] Punishments inflicted by the Romans on Jews also suggest violent

2. The Roman military power in the newly subdued province must have, since the year 70, been distributed all over the country (see *Wars*, VII, 6, 1), and, we should expect, could, if it wanted, have reached robbers near the important town of Lydda without difficulty. Though there is no evidence for the places of garrisons, numerous or small, Lydda was certainly one of them.[1] R. Joḥanan b. Zakkai had conversations with a Roman official called in *jer. Synh.*, I, 19 c, 16, Antoninus hegemon; I, 19 d, 3, Antigonos hegemon; I, 19b, 18, Angatos hegemon; *Num. r.*, 4, 9, Hongatos; *Bekhor.*, 5 a, Kontrakos the ruler[2]; in *Sifrê Deut.*, 351, Agnito shegemon, who asked R. Gamaliel a question. Hegemon does not necessarily denote the governor of Judaea; he may have been the commander of the garrison in Jamnia, and this all the more as none of the few governors known suits the name, nor any Greek or Roman name has so far been found to cover the form preserved in the Hebrew sources.[3] Jamnia was to the Roman administration of special importance on account of its imperial stores of produce. For in *Tos. Damm.*, I, 13, we read: R. Josê says: The rule mentioned applies to private stores only, but in the stores of the emperors we

acts in Judaea. A Jew in prison freed without witnesses the childless widow of his brother from marrying him (*Jebam.*, XII, 4 and 105 b, bottom), and R. Akiba declared it valid. Originally the rabbis said: When one goes away in a collarium and asks that a bill of divorce should be written for his wife, it should be written and delivered; later they added: a man who goes on a sea journey or with a caravan. R. Simeon Ṣhezuri added: a man who is dangerously ill, *Gitt.*, VI, 5. Now this disciple of R. Tarfon knew already the first additions to the original rule, so that this must have belonged at the latest to the time of his teacher. Executions, see in *Semaḥ.*, II, 11, 13. Galilean Jews suspected of murder came to R. Tarfon and asked for shelter, but he refused, *Nidd.*, 61 a, bottom.

[1] R. 'Aibo's statement about hostile fortresses in Palestine, p. 24, note 2 ff., must not be adduced, for he lived in the fourth century.

[2] Here *Rashi* and *Tosafoth* read R. Gamaliel instead of R. Joḥanan.

[3] See Grätz in *MGWJ*, 1885, XXXIV, 17 ff.; Bacher, *Tannaiten*, I, 36; Krauss, *Lehnwörter*, II, 106. *Midrash haGadol Deut.*, 33; *Midrasch Tannaim*, 215, read in the *Sifrê* passage: Agrippas hegemon asked R. Joḥanan b. Zakkai.

go as to the origin of the corn by the majority of it. R. Jehudah says: This applies to stores of Jews and non-Jews, but in stores of Jews and Samaritans we go by the majority of the produce. The rabbis then said to R. Josê: As you have told us concerning the stores of Jamnia before the war that the corn there was not certainly tithed, and most of the people who delivered there corn were Samaritans, we see that in the stores in Palestine into which corn is brought from abroad, as the stores of Regeb, all goes by the measure of the corn. R. Joshua b. Kaposai said that from the rules concerning the stores in Jamnia he derived a halachic lesson. Into those stores the taxes were delivered prescribed to be in kind, as *Tos. Damm.*, VI, 3, 4, clearly states: He who rents a field from a Samaritan, gives him the rent in kind after separating the tithes, then he weighs into the stores, he weighs to the centurion and then gives it to him. A Jew must not say to a non-Jew or a Samaritan or some one not trustworthy in tithing: Take 200 zuzs and weigh for me into the stores; but he should tell him: Free me from the stores.[1] The stores in Jamnia continued for a long time and existed still about the year 200. When once on the road, Rabbi and R. Josê b. R. Jehudah saw a non-Jew coming towards them; when he asked them who they were, what their occupation was, and where they were going, they replied: We are Jews and business men, and are going to buy wheat from the stores of Jamnia.[2] Here, then, produce could be bought

[1] 'Instead of me from the stores' cannot be correct, as the continuation clearly shows; cf. the Baraitha in *'Ab. zar.*, 71 a: A Jew must not ask a non-Jew to enter for him into the stores; see Rashi.

[2] From an economic point of view *Tos. Damm.*, I, 11, is very instructive: He who buys produce from a ship in Joppé or in Caesarea must give tithe. R. Jehudah said: The produce on the shore (?) of Jishub and of Antipatris and in the market of Patros was at first declared not certainly tithed, because it generally came from the King mountains; but now our rabbis said... Jishub was a Samaritan place (Neubauer, *Chronique Samaritaine*, 19), further south was Antipatris, so that the unknown Patros was further south. We learn that Judaea and the places in the central range north of Judaea exported produce via Joppé and to the three places.

by anybody. It need hardly be pointed out that such stores were supervised by officers, as the centurion mentioned, and other officials, and guarded by soldiers; the Kontarikos who discussed a question with R. Joḥanan b. Zakkai could have been a centurion of the stores.[1] Ben-Dama told his uncle R. Ishmael that in a dream both his jaws fell off, and R. Ishmael interpreted it to mean: Two Roman soldiers devised evil against you, but died (*Berakh.*, 56 b). Neither the place, nor the soldiers, nor the kind of device are defined, and it may be, that in order to confiscate his property, they wanted to accuse him of some invented crime,[2] as happened to the nephews of R. Joḥanan b. Zakkai in *B. bathra*, 10 a.[3] Jerusalem was a Roman camp, with the greater part of the Tenth Legion and all its usual following stationed there, and similarly other important places must have had garrisons.

3. The administrative military centres seem to have had Roman courts of justice. For R. Tarfon[4] says in

[1] The occasional visit of stratiotai in the school of Jamnia in the days of R. Gamaliel who came to learn the law of the Jews, *Sifrê Deut.*, 344, 143 b; *jer. B. kam.*, IV, 4 b, 29; b. 38 a, proves nothing for a garrison in the town.

[2] In an Aramaic story in *Ta'an.*, 21 a, the Jews sent through Naḥum of Gimzo a box of precious stones as a gift to the emperor; the Roman governor is meant. R. Joshi'a, R. Ishmael's disciple, in *ARN*, XXXVIII, 57 a, says that owing to neglect in giving priestly dues and tithes the skies withhold dew and rain, and the people is handed over to the government. This is taken from life, and refers to Roman confiscations of property.

[3] The presence of soldiers constituted a danger for Jewish women, as the case before R. Ḥaninah in *jer. Nedar.*, XI, 42 d, 58, shows: When once soldiers came into a city, the wife of a priest came to the beth-din and complained that a soldier had embraced and assaulted her; but the rabbis permitted her to continue to eat of her husband's priestly due. Also the *Mishnah Nedar.*, XI, 12, reflects such a danger. First the rabbis said: In three cases a woman must be divorced and receive her marriage settlement: when she says to her husband, I am defiled for you, God is between us, and I am removed from the Jews. Later the rabbis altered that rule in order that a woman should not commit adultery because she wants to marry somebody else. It seems that violation of women and persuading them to leave Judaism reflects Roman times.

[4] *She'iltoth*, בראשיה, read R. Meir, which is merely a misreading of the form ר"ט; *Midrash haGadol* to Exod. xxi also has R. Tarfon, and for agoras ארכיות.

Gitt., 88 b: Wherever you find agoras of non-Jews, even if their judgments are the same as of the Jews, you must not apply to them. Also R. Eleazar b. 'Azarjah in *Mekhiltha* on 21, 1, takes a stand against applying to these courts, and R. Akiba refers to deeds made at non-Jewish offices (*Gitt.*, 11 a; *Tos.*, I, 4).[1] R. Joḥanan b. Zakkai refers to human judges who can be appeased by gifts (*Berakh.*, 28 b). This seems to point to his experience with Roman judges in Judaea.[2] To such, as R. Tarfon's strong warning shows, Jews were inclined to apply, probably because the Roman officials suggested it to them and such courts were everywhere near at hand.[3]

[1] Otherwise the Jews had their own jurisdiction in civil cases and the right to impose fines, as the judgments of R. Akiba show (p. 39 ff.), and also the statement of Rabh in *Synh.*, 13 b, 14 a, that if R. Jehudah b. Baba during the Hadrianic persecutions had not ordained five disciples, the law about fines had been forgotten in Israel. There were no courts for capital punishment, in spite of Origen's remark to the contrary; for R. Akiba and R. Tarfon say in *Makk.*, I, 10, if they had been on a Synedrion, nobody would have ever been executed. The past tense clearly shows that in their times no such court was in existence. Scholars frequently point out that the rabbis applied the ban to force recalcitrant parties to obey their judgments. But as evidence not one single occurrence could be adduced; for all cases reported concern rabbis who either persisted in their individual teachings and had to be banned, or such as had disobeyed the orders of R. Jehudah haNassi.

[2] In Jellinek's *beth-haMidrasch*, I, 1; *Esther r.*, introduction, § 9, 'Abba Gorjon, in the name of R. Gamaliel, says: Since untrue judges increased, false witnesses increased; since delatores (informers) increased, the robbing of people's money (confiscations) increased, . . . since the beloved children provoked their father in heaven, he raised over them a wicked king to punish them. This statement, obviously picturing the times of R. Gamaliel, reveals sad conditions in Judaea under Roman rule, especially the evil of informers. Perhaps R. Eleazar b. 'Azarjah's sentence against the evil tongue in *Makk.*, 23 a, refers to the same: He who speaks evil language and he who receives evil language and he who gives false testimony, deserve to be thrown before dogs. See Bacher, *Tannaiten*, I, 91, 1.

[3] Not merely in Caesarea where R. Eliezer was once tried on the béma by a hegemon as judge, *Kohel. r.*, 1, 8, 3; *'Abod. z.*, 16 b; *Tos. Ḥull.*, II, 24, and R. Akiba by Tineius Rufus, Bacher, *Tannaiten*, I, 287, and *Midr. Prov.*, 9, 2. R. Eliezer's statement made in connexion with his trial in *'Ab. zar.*, 17 a, on Prov. v. 8 b: Draw not near to the entrance of her house, to the government, also warns against relations with the Romans. But the two parallels quoted do not contain that word.

Not merely the wealthy Jews felt attracted by them, but also the poor who seem to have received support from the Romans. For in an interpretation of Prov. xiv. 34: The lovingkindness of the nations is sin, asked by R. Joḥanan b. Zakkai of his disciples, R. Eliezer says: All kindness done by non-Jews is sin to them, for they do such only to boast; R. Joshua said: They do such only to prolong their rule. The latter explanation clearly shows that the Romans were referred to, whom also the interpretation of R. Eleazar of Modeim fits, that they practise charity only to abuse us.[1] Both rabbis presuppose that the Romans support Jews by alms.[2] In this way and by persuasion the representatives of the Roman government and other non-Jews tried to win over the Jews of Judaea. For R. Akiba, in a dialogue between Israel and the nations, makes the latter say: Why do you die for your God, and are killed for Him? You are bright and valiant; come and mix with us.[3]

The emperor owned property in Judaea; not only 800 veterans received land in Emmaus near Jerusalem (*Wars*, VII,6,6), but also other property must have been in Roman hands. Apart from the agadic, but certainly not groundless reference to Hadrian's vineyard of 18 by 18 miles (*jer. Ta'an.*, IV, 69 a, 18) which was manured by the blood of

[1] *B. bathra*, 10 b; *Pesik.*, 12 b; Bacher, *Tannaiten*, I, 34, 4. Of Roman charity in Palestine about the year 300 speaks R. Jisḥak in *Pesik.*, 95 b: The governors go out to the villages, plunder the farmers, return to their town and say: Call the poor together, for we want to give them charity. In *Midrash haGadol* on Deut. vii. 26, quoted by Dr. Schechter in his *'Agadath Canticum*, p. 71, the kindness of the nations in Prov. xiv. 34 is referred to the Romans building public and other baths for the poor and rich, but leaving there a place for worshipping idols and for immoral women. But there is beside a doubtful reference of R. Gamaliel none mentioning such institutions in Judaea before the year 135.

[2] See also *Tos. Sotah*, XIV, 10: Since the number of those increased who accepted charity from non-Jews, non-Jews began to increase and Jews to decrease, and the latter have in the world no pleasure. If this statement could be dated, it would be an instructive parallel to the above passage.

[3] *Mekhil.* on 15, 2; *Mekhil. R. Simeon*, 60; Bacher, *Tannaiten*, I, 285, 4.

the slain of Betthar, a very instructive address of R. Joḥanan b. Zakkai (*Mekhil.*, 19, 1, p. 61 b) refers to imperial vineyards. He said to some Jews, as representing the whole nation: You would not pay the tax of one beka' per head to God, now you pay 15 shekels to the government of your enemies; you would not repair the roads and the markets for the pilgrims, now you repair את הבורגסין ואת הבורגמין for those who go up to the vineyards of emperors.[1] As R. Joḥanan spoke to all the Palestinian Jews, there must have been in Judaea several such vineyards. Schiller[2] states that soldiers stationed in a Roman province were in peace engaged in draining work and in planting vineyards, the latter especially to facilitate the necessary supply of wine for the soldiers. In connexion with such imperial plantations the Jews in Judaea had probably to do compulsory work of various kinds; as R. Joḥanan's contrast of past and present shows, in the first instance they had to keep up the roads. There is express evidence that the balsam plantations of 'En-gedi were imperial property and were farmed by the fiscus,[3] and the balsam was sold by the fiscus.[4] The same applied

[1] In *'Agadath Canticum*, 1, 6, a similar but anonymous passage occurs: You would not guard the Temple as required, now they guard the great fortress. Schechter, p. 58, thinks it a corruption of the *Mekhiltha* passage, but there is hardly a trace of it here. If שומרין were from שוקלין, the sentence would be clearer: They have to pay taxes to Caesarea or Rome.

[2] *Geschichte der röm. Kaiserzeit*, I, 881.

[3] Galenus, vol. XIV, p. 25, ed. Kühn; Marquardt, *Röm. Staatsverwaltung*, II², 258.

[4] Galenus, XIV, 7; Pliny, *Nat. Hist.*, 12, 111, 113, 123. In whose hands 'En-gedi had been before the war is not evident. Though it was one of the eleven toparchies (*Wars*, III, 3, 5), but not mentioned as such by Pliny (V, 14, 70), and though Eusebius, *Onom.*, 254, terms it a very great Jewish place, its plantations may have been already before the year 70 in Roman hands. During the revolution the sicarii of Masada attacked it (*Wars*, IV, 7, 2) in the night of Passover, scattered the population and drove it from the town, and women and children about 700 were killed. All the villages around Masada were laid waste and the whole district made desolate. It is difficult to see why the sicarii should have killed Jewish women and children, as they could have taken the victuals which they wanted from the women. It seems, 'En-gedi was either in favour of peace or partly inhabited by Romans.

to Jericho, as Pliny in his note on the balsam-bush says (XII, 25, 112): Servit nunc haec ac tributa pendit cum sua gente, presupposing that both balsam gardens had the same political position, as in fact he says (113): Seritque nunc eum fiscus.[1]

4. The Roman taxes weighed heavily upon all the Jews. For even those to whom, as to Josephus, their property was returned by Titus and Vespasian, had to pay taxes, and Josephus himself reports (*Vita*, 76) that the Emperor Domitian freed him from the taxes of his property in Palestine, which was the greatest distinction for any one.[2] The tax to be paid in addition to the poll-tax varied in various provinces,[3] a fifth or a seventh of the produce, in kind or in money, according to the value of the field. What tax R. Joḥanan b. Zakkai meant by 15 shekels, the passage quoted does not suggest. Nor does the list of Jewish taxes in a papyrus from Arsinoë of the 5th year of Vespasian[4] constitute a parallel to it. Though the Jews are there distinguished from the bulk of the native population, and already children pay the Jewish tax by head and year, 8 drachmae and 2 oboloi, and in addition to it 1 drachma ἀπαρχῆς, and again poll-tax, altogether about 40 drachmae, yet no relation of those taxes is visible to the Judaean didrachma.[5] The fixed amount mentioned by R. Joḥanan shows that the tax was not varying according to the produce of a field,

[1] Cp. Hölscher, *Judäa in pers. u. hell. Zeit*, 49.

[2] The version of R. Neḥunjah b. Hakanah's sentence in 2 *ARN*, XXXII, 34 b: From him who takes upon him the yoke of the Torah, the yoke of the government and of business is removed, and upon him who shakes off the yoke of the Torah, the yoke of the government and of business is imposed, suggests that scholars were exempted from taxes, regular or irregular. See Krakauer in *MGWJ*, 1874, XXIII, 60 ff.; *RÉJ*, 1912, LXIV, 60, which, however, refer to the edicts of the emperors of the fourth century, as perhaps *ARN*; *'Aboth*, III, 8, does not contain the 'yoke of the government'.

[3] Marquardt, *Staatsverwaltung*, II^2, 222.

[4] C. Wessely, *Studien z. Palaeogr. u. Papyruskunde*, 1901, 9.

[5] Schürer, *Geschichte*, III^4, 46 ff.

but a fixed contribution, perhaps a minimum paid on leasing one's own field from the Roman governor. The tax in kind to be paid into the Roman corn stores to the centurion (p. 58), was probably the income-tax or the annona. The forced labour mentioned by R. Joḥanan at בורנמין seems to have concerned fields, for the nearest word, of which it is evidently a corruption, בורגנין is found in connexion with fields, though only in statements after the year 135.[1] In addition to those, a tax of food, bread, drink, and clothes was demanded, called cellaria,[2] which, according to R. Ḥaninah's, the vice high priest's description (p. 42), was felt very heavily owing to the great poverty after the War. R. Gamaliel gives further information about Roman impositions (*ARN*, XXVIII, 43a): By four things the government consumes (property), by customs, baths, theatres, and annonae.[3] But very little is known about duties in Judaea in our period, except the Baraitha in *B. kam.*, 113a: One must not put on garments of mixed stuffs, not even over ten other garments, in order to defraud duty; R. Akiba, opposing the view, says: One must not defraud duty; R. Simeon, in R. Akiba's name, says: one may defraud duty.[4] But even this is doubtful; none of the other passages about custom, *Semaḥ.*, II, 9; *Nedar.*, III, 4; *Tos.*, II, 2, can with probability be referred to Judaea before the year 135. About Roman public baths, nothing is preserved in Jewish sources, though it is probable that for the Roman garrisons and officials such were built; R. Eleazar b. 'Arakh settled in Emmaus on account of its good water and its baths (p. 21 ff.). Even less is known about theatres

[1] Krauss in *Berliner-Hoffmann's Magazin*, XIX, 110, without sufficient evidence applies the words to military fortifications.

[2] Marquardt, l. c., 232.

[3] The wording is doubtful; see Schechter, 12, who quotes a version במסאות, altars.

[4] *Tosafoth Zebaḥ.*, 91b, quoting from memory attribute the first anonymous sentence to R. Akiba, but his name is even in the second part doubtful; see Rabbinowicz and R. Isaiah Trani the elder in *JQR*, IV, 93 ff.

in Judaea, as the only reference in R. Neḥunjah b. Hakanah's sentence in *jer. Berakh.*, IV, 7 d, 39, is not to be found in the parallel Baraitha in *Berakh.*, 28 b (p. 31, note 1). And it is not probable that the Romans built in Judaea theatres, as no halachic or agadic reference deals with such. Nor is there any trace of any form of idols and idolatry which the rabbis would have certainly discussed for the guidance of the school and the people.[1] Jerusalem and Emmaus, important military stations, must naturally have had some Roman temple, just as the maritime cities inhabited by non-Jews.[2] Akko had a bath of Aphroditê (*'Ab. z.*, III, 4), and Caesarea heathen sacrifices (*Hull.*, 39 b; *Tos.*, II, 13). R. Akiba says (*Synh.*, 65 b) that as a heathen obtains by fasting the spirit of his god, how much more should a Jew by fasting obtain the spirit of God; but our sins prevent it. And when Zonen asks R. Akiba his opinion about healings by sleeping in a heathen temple,[3] the master gives an explanation of such cures; in both cases he presupposes the existence of heathen worship in his neighbourhood. Either in Jamnia, where Roman officials resided, or more probably in Caesarea or Askalon, the seats of various heathen worships, R. Akiba and Zonen could have observed those rites. Askalon had a market which the rabbis used to frequent (*Tos. 'Ahil.*, XVIII, 18), and was a city which R. Gamaliel

[1] Schlatter, *Tage Trajans*, 68, states that the Roman legion brought its cult with it, and refers to the stone still standing in the Nebi Daud gate in Jerusalem set by the legio III Cyrenaica in 116 for the welfare and victory of Trajan and the Roman people to Jupiter Optumus Maxumus Sarapis.

[2] In *Midrasch Tannaim*, 58; 2 *ARN*, XXXI, 33 b ff., R. Joḥanan b. Zakkai says: Be not hasty in pulling down the altars of heathens that thou shouldst not have to rebuild them with thy hand; pull not down any of bricks that they should not ask thee to rebuild them of stone; nor of stone that they should not ask thee to rebuild them of wood. This shows that there were in Judaea heathen altars which some Jews were eager to pull down; but it is possible and even probable to refer such statements to the time before the War. Cf. also the parallel in *Meg.*, 31 b; *Tos. 'Ab. z.*, I, 19; Bacher, *Tannaiten*, II, 425, 3.

[3] *'Abod. z.*, 55 a; Bacher, *Tannaiten*, I, 294.

with Akylas visited (*Tos. Mikw.*, VI, 3);[1] and where R. Joshua was on a political mission (*Sabb.*, 127 b; 2 *ARN*, XIX, 21 a), and where Asklepios was worshipped (Schürer, II, 24).

5. A few words have to be added about the presence of non-Jews in Judaea. The land having been declared the private property of Vespasian, and a million of its inhabitants having fallen or been sold in the War, it would seem the most natural thing that non-Jews, Romans, and non-Jewish Palestinians, flocked in great numbers into the country and leased property. But no information to that effect has come down, except a reference to property in the possession of a matrona who gave Hyrkanos, R. Eliezer's son, yearly 300 kors, tithe from her produce.[2] She was probably the wife or widow of a wealthy Roman or Syrian in the neighbourhood of Lydda, as we find a matrona in Askalon (*Sabb.*, 127 b, above). R. Joḥanan b. Zakkai was asked by a non-Jew the difference between Jewish and non-Jewish festivals (*Deut. r.*, 7, 7); and as he enumerates Kalendae, Saturnalia, and Kratesis, he is a Roman official, provided the enumeration is no imitation of R. Meir's in *'Abodah z.*, I, 2. There was a non-Jewish laundry to which R. Gamaliel of Jamnia gave his linen to wash, as reported by R. Eleazar b. R. Ṣadok.[3] R. Joḥanan b. Nuri refers to a religious question raised in Jamnia about a hen, and his colleagues remind him that several non-Jews in Jamnia prepared hens for food (*Nidd.*, 50 b). An incestuous heathen woman came to R. Eliezer and R. Joshua to be admitted into Judaism (*Kohel. r.*, 1, 8). A wealthy woman, Veluria, who owned slaves, became a proselyte[4]; she lived in Jamnia or Lydda, where she

[1] R. Eliezer referred to a man in Askalon who honoured his father greatly, *Kidd.*, 31 a; *jer. Pe'ah*, I, 15 c, 18; *Pesik. r.*, XXIV, 123 b.

[2] *Jer. Sotah*, III, 19 a, 7; in the parallel *Joma*, 66 b, only a woman is mentioned.

[3] *Sabb.*, I, 9; *Baraitha*, 19 a; *Tos.*, I, 22.

[4] *Mekhil.*, 12, 48, p. 18 a; *Jebam.*, 46 a; *Gerim*, II, 4.

asked R. Gamaliel about a contradiction in the Bible (*Rosh ha-Shan.*, 17 b, bottom). R. Josê, the priest, a former disciple of R. Johanan b. Zakkai, who was with R. Gamaliel when that question was asked, was in his observance of the Sabbath so strict that, to avoid a profanation of it, he did not allow any letter of his to be found in the hands of a non-Jew (*Sabb.*, 19 a). Where they lived is not indicated. A non-Jew brought on a Jewish holy day fish to R. Gamaliel which he would not accept (*Beṣah*, III, 2). But all these references prove nothing as to an influx of non-Jews into Judaea after the War. The long preparations of the Jews for the great rising under bar-Kochba unnoticed by non-Jews, confirm the impression that beside the few and scattered officials of the Roman government very few non-Jews lived among the Jewish population in Judaea.

6. The main results of these lengthy investigations into the economic conditions of Judaea from the destruction of Jerusalem by Titus in the year 70 to the bar-Kochba war in the year 133 are the following. In the long war from 66 to 70 the Romans destroyed, besides Jerusalem, many towns, forts, and villages, and depopulated many other places. But as the resistance of the country had not been sufficiently organized by the leaders of the revolution, many important places surrendered to the Romans and were spared. From Josephus and the Talmudic literature the names of several of those can be traced. Though a million of Jews perished in Jerusalem, over forty thousand of its citizens went over to the Romans during the siege, and having been spared constituted with the Jews, spared in the country, the population of Judaea after the catastrophe. Among them were many priests of high standing, and nobles and wealthy landowners, some with their wives and children, who, as a reward for their surrender, received their former property from Titus and Vespasian. Others bought or leased land, often their own, from the emperor

who had declared the whole of Judaea his private property, so that a considerable portion of the country was farmed in the usual way. Among the survivors were several wealthy rabbis, and having their property restored, were landowners and supported their own schools. The laws concerning the priestly dues and the sabbatical year were mostly observed, and the poor without land and money were supported, especially in years of drought. The representatives of the Roman administration in Judaea interfered little with the Jews, only the various taxes were heavy and retarded the recovery of the country and its population. Still, it progressed so rapidly that in two generations a hundred thousand Jews could again rise in several hundred places of Judaea against the Roman rule. The best known towns were Lydda and Jamnia; they had received from Vespasian new inhabitants from other Judaean places which had surrendered to the Romans. Jamnia had Roman corn stores for receiving taxes delivered in kind, and it was the seat of the highest religious body, the beth-din. Lydda had many wealthy inhabitants, among them scholars at the head of schools for adults. Both towns are often referred to in the Talmud, and the material preserved affords some insight into the life of Jewish places. Around them were several Jewish towns and villages of greater and smaller importance. The discussion of many details of private and public life, of men and women, of property and farming, of schools and scholars, of goods and trade, of towns and villages, and of Roman rule and violence, affords additional information about the conditions in Judaea and the life of all sections of its population from the year 70 to 135.

www.ingramcontent.com/pod-product-compliance
Lightning Source LLC
Chambersburg PA
CBHW061510040426
42450CB00008B/1542
9781606086872